THE
UNICORN
PATH

THE ONE WITH THE MOST
UNICORNS WINS

By

BART DUNNE

Copyright © 2021 Bart Dunne
The Unicorn Path
Mystic Canyon Publishing
Los Angeles, CA
ISBN: 978-1-7351673-5-0

TABLE OF CONTENTS

SECTION I

HOW TO BUILD A GREAT TEAM AND DOMINATE THE COMPETITION

THE UNICORN PATH

An Introduction

This book provides a detailed and executable system for business owners to dominate their competition. The Unicorn Path version of domination does not involve violence or subterfuge. Unicorn Path domination results from building a team that is dramatically better than the competition. If you choose to walk the Unicorn Path with passion and commitment, you will build a vastly superior team that will generate:

- Increased revenue
- Higher margins
- Greater profitability
- Amazing customer retention
- Dramatically improved employee retention
- Premier recruiting
- The happiness that comes from sustainable success and a great culture

It has been said that when you are being chased by a bear you, do not need to be faster than the bear, you just need to be faster than the slowest person being chased. If you are looking for minor incremental improvement (being slightly faster than the slowest guy), this is the wrong book for you. This book is for companies that want to obliterate their competition by having a team that's vastly more effective than the competition. Close your eyes for a minute and imagine what it would be like to have a team that is 2, 3 or maybe even 10 times better than your competitors. To keep the metaphor going, this book is about running faster than the bear.

Building a high-performance team requires relentless focus and determination. The Unicorn Path is based on dramatic improvement. Improvement = Change, Change = Discomfort. You will not make it if you are not relentless. You are working to dominate your competition by building a team of high performers. The only way to get there is to bear down and power through.

Why the Path?

Walking the Unicorn Path will be constantly used to describe the process for obtaining individual and team high performance. The path is not straight, and the path is not easy. You will get knocked off the path—it is inevitable when you become involved with difficult tasks. Success comes from two things:

- Your resolve to fight to get back on the path.
- The support you receive from others to get back on the path.

Disengagement

A disengaged employee is someone who usually does not enjoy their work. They generally do the bare minimum and do not put in the extra effort.

This disengagement problem really hit home for me when I read a Gallup study that indicated that 30% of all employees are engaged (interested/involved) in their jobs while 70% of all employees were disengaged. While the ratio between engaged and disengaged varied in subsequent studies, the original ratio still holds up as reasonable. The study covered all types of businesses, and the 30/70 ratio applies to both blue-collar and white-collar jobs.

In 2019 the outplacement firm of Challenger, Gray and Christmas estimated that employers lost $13.3 billion in productivity from the year's NCAA Basketball Tournament.

Based on the huge cost of lost productivity due to a basketball tournament, imagine the trillions of dollars lost due to poor productivity from the disengaged.

The Causes of Disengagement

Nearly every company understands the benefit of having engaged employees. Nearly every job seeker hopes for a job that they can love and prosper. Despite these mutually beneficial objectives, only 30% of all people working today are interested in their jobs. The rest are lost in the abyss of disengagement. Here are my two theories as to why disengagement is so prevalent:

- Companies treat employees like commodities – To paraphrase the amazing deceased comic George Carlin, employers pay just enough so that workers will not quit, and employees work just hard enough so that they won't be fired. The idea of a fair day's pay for a fair day's work does not work. It takes more than fair pay to create a high performer.
- Companies do not know how to build great employees – Most companies do not have the slightest idea how to build a high-performance team. This book lays out a clear path to building a high-performance organization.

Win the Game That Most Aren't Playing

According to OfficeVibe.com, a website devoted to employee engagement, "90% of leaders think a strategy to enhance employee engagement would help their companies, but only 25% percent of companies have a strategy to improve employee engagement." While I am a big fan of OfficeVibe.com, you do not need to trust this percentage. Assess it yourself. Think about your past experiences, think about other businesses in your network, think about your competition. If you agree that OfficeVibe.com's 25% is even close to a reasonable number, get angry, get passionate, and get started on the path to crushing your competition.

It gets even better. Most of the 25% percent of the companies fighting the battle against disengagement have poorly implemented and/or executed talent development strategies. Think of playing the most lucrative game in all of business and how easy it is to win when only 25% of the participants play.

Being Engaged Is Not Good Enough

It is indisputable that employees who are engaged are more effective than employees who are disengaged, but passion is not enough.

The Foundation of a High Performer (Unicorn) is a commitment to:

- Making themselves better
- Making others around them better
- Making their companies better

Engaged beats disengaged →Unicorn high performers beat engaged.

In Chapter 1, we will delve further into the key attributes of a Unicorn High Performer.

Choose Your Battle

Walking the Unicorn Path is hard. It is not quadratic equation hard—there are no super sophisticated theories. The odds are good that you have previously considered everything that is being put forth in this book. I think of myself as an idea chef. I did not create any new ingredients; I just created a new recipe.

The hard part of walking the Unicorn Path is that it involves change. Change is the less comfortable synonym for Improvement. Since every page in this book is committed to improvement, every page in this book is likely to bring the discomfort of change.

Walking the Unicorn Path involves reorienting every aspect of what you have done your whole life. The Unicorn Path does not mean throwing away your old ways, it involves improving your old ways, and unfortunately, it is harder than you think.

It boils down to this – if you passionately embrace change and commit to walking the Unicorn Path, you will dominate the competition. If you do not passionately embrace change, you will stay the same. It is up to you to decide if the challenge of change is worth it.

This Book has Two Sections

The first section of this book is geared toward giving companies the tools to create a high-performance environment. The second section of the book, The Unicorn Principles, weaves together 17 principles to create a high-performance operating system for ambitious employees.

I have gotten a lot of feedback about the high number of principles. I heard, "Why 17? Can you trim it to 3 or 4 to make the principles easier to digest?" My answer is that I wish there was an easier path toward creating high performers. I recognize that fully embracing 17 principles is an incredible challenge, but the dynamics that sentence 70% of all workers to a disengaged career are well established and extremely powerful. Unfortunately, I could not find the equivalent of a weight loss pill or a phone app to make things better. My simple but challenging solution is for employees to achieve greatness by passionately and relentlessly embracing change within an environment of strong support and systematic excellence.

The Unicorn Principles are also available in a separate book that you can hand to an ambitious employee to put them on the path to becoming a high-performing employee.

The End of the Beginning

This is a short but dense book; it is more like flourless chocolate cake than angel food cake. It was my objective to provide a valuable takeaway on every page. Skim if you must, but I do not want you to miss any tools that will help you dominate your competition.

This is the first book I have written. I was an accounting major, not an English major. While I received exceptional editing assistance, I would like to request that you persevere through every grammatical, syntax, and continuity issues. Also, I ask for your indulgence with my repetition. Based on my personal experience, I believe that once is not enough for critical points.

My biased recommendation is for you to read the book from the first page to the last before you decide whether to embrace the immense challenge of change and to decide whether to commit to the Unicorn Path.

CHAPTER 1

Defining A Unicorn

For this book, the intended meaning for Unicorn is **someone that is highly desirable but difficult to find or obtain.** High-performance employees are the Unicorns of businesses. Unlike the mythical horned horse, these Unicorns exist.

As previously mentioned in the introduction, the fundamental aspects of a Unicorn are:

- A Commitment to making themselves better.
- A Commitment to making others around them better.
- A Commitment to making their companies better.

Other Characteristics of a Unicorn

- They love money but place a higher value on happiness.
- They care more about others than themselves.
- They seek to give more than they get.
- They want to win as a team.
- They can compel others to action (lead).
- They know how to provide tough feedback in an effective manner.

- They gear their emotional operating system to focus on optimizing their results.
- They overcome setbacks and recover quickly.

Pedigree is Nice for Dogs but Not for Unicorns

It does not matter who someone knows or where someone went to school. Everyone can master the Path; it is purely a matter of commitment and desire.

Good Characteristics that are not Enough

There are many qualities that are valuable in the workplace that fall short of high-performance greatness. Here are three examples of well-regarded characteristics that fall short of the Unicorn Path:

Hard Work Is Not Enough – Hard work is a wonderful trait, but a lone wolf who does not work in a team environment is not a Unicorn. Also, a sustainable work pace is critical for long-term high employee performance.

High Effectiveness Is Not Enough – There are many instances of highly effective employees who are not interested in personal improvement and/or working within a team environment.

Being Extremely Nice is Not Enough – It is a great pleasure to walk into a workplace and receive a big smile and a warm greeting. Happiness and culture are critical in a Unicorn Path environment, but a nice employee who does not embrace change is not a high performer.

Companies that have a lot of hard workers, highly effective employees, and nice people are likely to have good success. Companies that have a lot of Unicorns along with hard workers, highly effective performers, and nice people will dominate their competition.

The Unicorn Path is designed to optimize, not diminish, the value of hard workers, highly effective employees, and very nice employees. We will get further into this in Chapter 4 – The Unicorn Conversion Plan.

A Unicorn Scorecard

The Unicorn Principles in the second half of this book provide a detailed listing of high performer attributes. The Unicorn Principles includes an accompanying workbook that allows high performers in training to track their progress. The workbook details performance progress and makes it easy to determine who wants to improve and who does not want to change.

Wrap Up

Having a clear definition of a high performer is the foundation for walking The Unicorn Path. Get clarity, get the right people, crush your competition.

CHAPTER 2

Great Employees are Worth More Than Great Customers

By stating that great employees are worth more than great customers, I am in no way advocating that Great Customers are not important. I am stating that a company can dominate its competition by deploying the same energy, commitment, and creativity to employee performance as they do to business development.

Companies will do extraordinary things to acquire great customers. I often ask entrepreneurs if they would hire a marching band or rent a hotel ballroom to obtain a great customer, and the answer is almost always yes. But when I ask if they would do the same as part of the recruiting process or employee motivation, I typically get a less enthusiastic answer.

To win the Employee Performance game, you need to consider that great employees are the key to your success:

- The time a great employee spends with your company is typically longer than the time a customer does business with your company.
- Great employees make it easier to get great customers.

- Great employees make it easier to keep great customers.
- Great employees increase customer value/margin.
- Great employees generate great referrals and online reviews.

Make Building a High-Performance Team Your #1 Strategic Initiative

Unless your company has an incredible R&D breakthrough or a patented process, the way to rise above the competition is to have a dramatically better team than the competition.

Seventy-five percent of your competition are not taking any meaningful steps to improve employee performance. The remaining competitors see the value in improved performance but are unlikely to have a focused and committed plan. Your top strategic initiative is a declaration of your Company's highest level of focus, commitment, and resources. Directing your most meaningful efforts toward building a high-performance team will be your single biggest competitive advantage.

Adopting high performance as your top initiative does not mean that you are abandoning other critical aspects of your strategic plan. The better your team, the better your Company will be able to handle multiple initiatives.

Here are some keys to implementing high performance as your top strategic initiative:

- Advertise it – Let everyone in your Company and everyone within earshot hear that your top commitment is winning by having exceptional people.
- Define it – Define high performance and make sure everyone knows your definition.

- Clarify it – Let everyone know what his or her role is in the process of building a high-performing team. Keep in mind that employees who are not Unicorns have a critical role in building a high-performance team.
- Commit to it – Document well-conceived goals and identify the critical resources necessary to build a high-performance team.
- Visualize it – Let everyone know your vision of a high-performance team and help each person in your Company build their personal version of a high-performance environment.
- Score It – Keep track of your progress.
- Be Relentless – In the absence of incredible persistence, even the most powerful initiatives lose steam and eventually wash away.

Make Employees an Investment not an Expense

The biggest mistake that your competition makes is treating their employees like an expense or a commodity. It is human nature to limit what we spend on expenses. When employees are being treated like commodities, they typically reciprocate by performing at the low performance levels expected from a commodity.

Contrast the natural inclination to minimize expenses with the inherent desire to optimize investments. By treating employees with the mindset of an investment, your company is expressing its recognition of their current value and their potential future value. We cherish and covet our investments, and we should do the same with employees. You and your employees both win when you are willing to invest in their success.

It is rare to have an investment that has a perfect incline of success. You will experience setbacks and disappointments building a high-performance team. Work to overcome your issues and maintain your investment perspective.

Value Drives Commitment, Commitment Drives Results

Money drives focus, motivation, and commitment. From the receptionist to the CEO, there is an incredible gap in value/profitability between the best, average, and worst at each position. Work to quantify the value of every position at your Company. It is a lot easier to passionately pursue recruiting if you know that the difference between a high performer and a mediocre performer is $20K in additional annual profit.

Typically, it is easiest to assess the value of a salesperson. For example, if the expectation is for a salesperson to have a $1 million quota, and the average gross profit is 35%, the salesperson will annually contribute $350K toward overhead and profit.

For positions that are challenging to quantify, build a process to estimate the value of a high performer vs. an average performer vs. a poor performer. Continue to assess and update the assumptions of your estimate. Take into consideration the value of happiness and strong culture.

Assigning values to performance levels for each position will add tremendous focus and commitment to your recruiting.

Reflection Time

If you choose to walk the Unicorn Path, you are in the high-performance employee building business. Having one Unicorn will make a dramatic impact on a Company. Two is even better, and know that the company with the most Unicorns wins. Once you win, do not stop. The more Unicorns you have, the better your life

CHAPTER 3

The Two Key Roles of a CEO

The CEO is typically a company's most valuable and talented employee. Accordingly, there is a lot of competition for a CEO's time. To build a Unicorn environment there are two key roles that a CEO should focus on:

Role #1 – Business Development – Companies that walk the Unicorn Path are building companies that create high performers. To retain Unicorns and optimize the resulting incredible competitive advantage, it is important to remove barriers to employee advancement. The more revenue opportunities generated, the more career opportunities available to Unicorns. Here are some business development activities to consider:

- Enhancing the sales organization
- Creating new revenue through strong customer referral programs
- Broadening existing product/service offerings
- Acquisitions of complementary business
- Acquisitions of businesses in new areas

Strong revenue generation is critical. If Unicorns start bumping their heads against a ceiling of opportunities, they will look elsewhere. Start fast, be diligent, and crush your competition.

Role #2 – Be a Company That is Worthy of Unicorns – you are building a team that is focused on excellence and change. You cannot build an excellent team if you do not have an excellent company. The quality of your Company's environment is also a competition. The best place to work will attract or retain the highest performers. CEOs should focus on crushing their competition by being the best place for the best people to work.

It is futile to build great performers if you are not committed to creating a great environment. It is like continuously filling a leaky bucket. You keep working to build a great team, and the great performers leak out to companies that have environments that match their values.

Chapter 7 focuses on the details of what it takes to attract and retain high performers.

Building a High-Performance Team

I did not include Strategic Initiative #1 as a primary role of the CEO. There is no doubt that CEOs have a critical role with building a high-performing team. Building a high-performance team is a Companywide initiative where every person in a company contributes to this initiative's success. CEOs should help develop and monitor the high-performance plan, but their focus is needed on creating an environment where high performers thrive.

The Path Isn't Straight

There will always be emergencies and distractions that clash with key objectives. Goals and initiatives do not guarantee results. Goals and initiatives indicate a committed plan focused on the most important activities. When enough time and effort is committed to an initiative, the initiative is likely achieved. The objective of Walking the

Unicorn Path is to dominate the competition. The more a CEO focuses his or her efforts on business development and building a great environment, the more likely your Company will successfully walk the Unicorn Path.

CHAPTER 4

The Unicorn Conversion Plan

The Gallup study on disengagement referenced in the introduction divides employees into engaged (30%) and disengaged (70%). The same study adds an actively disengaged subcategory (25% of all employees and about 1/3rd of the disengaged). The Unicorn Path divides employees into the following groups:

Unicorns – this category has already been defined in Chapter 1. Unicorns make everything in a company better.

Unicorns in Training – Unicorns in Training lack expert skills and are still learning the Unicorn Principles to excel as high-performing employees.

Craftsmen (and women) – This is the most effective category of the disengaged. Craftspeople are critical to the success of most companies. Craftspeople have great expertise and take pride in what they do. Examples of craftspeople include a partner in a law firm that has carved out a nice niche in a component of the law or a master mechanic at a car dealership. Craftspeople are disengaged because they lack overall passion for their organization, and they are resistant to the change that comes from personal improvement. Regardless of how many Unicorns your Company builds, Craftspeople are critical to your Company's ongoing success. They need to be valued and supported.

Tourists – Tourists are employees that have little passion for their jobs. They are temporary visitors that move on when the time is right. They are in the coast mode like the C students in high school. Tourists work to pay the bills and fund their interests outside of work.

Terrorists – Terrorists are what The Gallup Study refers to as the actively disengaged. I refer to the actively disengaged as terrorists because they attack your Company's culture and passionately work to recruit others to join them. According to the Gallup study, the actively disengaged represent approximately 25% of an average company's workforce. In my experience, the number of terrorists varies, but the overall 25% makes sense.

This is the recommended conversion plan for each employee category:

CEO – nothing happens without the CEO's commitment to passionately walk The Unicorn Path and vigorously live The Unicorn Principles. The change required can be mentally challenging, and the time commitment is similar to an MBA class for at least a year.

Walking the Unicorn Path is likely worth it for a CEO who is passionate about dominating their marketplace and/or building a powerful succession strategy, but CEOs who are already living a great life might find The Path too challenging.

Other Leaders – Successful Senior management is comprised of two major categories:

- Leaders who embrace change and improvement.

- Leaders who have fought and scraped to achieve their success and view change as a threat to their hard-earned success.

Change-oriented executives can make excellent champions for the program. Champions are critical to implementing The Unicorn Path. Change-oriented executives will dive into the Unicorns in Training Program and be the vanguard for a strong Unicorn Path implementation.

Do not force The Unicorn Path on leaders who do not embrace change (similar to craftspeople referred to later in this section). They are great contributors to your Company's success, and the massive change of The Unicorn Path could cause them great stress. Solicit their critical feedback and welcome their participation in any aspect of the process. Many change-resistant executives will join you on The Unicorn Path once they get comfortable with the process. Give them the patience and time that their good work has earned them.

Unicorns – Even though they are high performers, a Unicorn's desire for improvement never stops. Provide Unicorns with customized programs to focus on key areas such as:

- Emotional intelligence
- Optimizing conversations
- Building trust
- Advanced team building

Unicorns should also continue using their Unicorn Principle workbooks to track improvement.

The topics and the opportunities for improvement are infinite.

Unicorn development will be addressed further in Chapter 9.

Unicorns in Training – The Unicorn Path offers, a 13-week Unicorn certification program. The objective of the program is to get trainees firmly on The Unicorn Path by providing a strong context of the 17 Principles. Upon certification, trainees participate with Unicorns in customized training programs designed to enhance their continued improvement.

Companies should also develop accelerated programs to provide Unicorns in Training with the necessary skills specific to their job. Skill development takes time and patience, but the faster a company builds Unicorns, the faster they will crush the competition.

Craftspeople – Leave them alone. Highly effective disengaged employees are extremely resistant to change. Suddenly thrusting change upon a Craftsperson will likely result in extreme stress and diminished performance. Let them know that The Unicorn Path is designed to dramatically improve their support and the company's success. Inform them that they are extremely valuable, and this process will not be a threat to their job status. Invite them to participate at their pace and let them know that they are welcome to fully join in the process should they choose to do so.

Tourists – Many companies have some genuinely nice tourists. There are countless reasons for a tourist to lose their passion for their job. Ultimately, you are working to replace tourists with Unicorns. Welcome tourists who are interested in becoming Unicorns but do not try to recruit them. Tourists are another category resistant to change.

Terrorists – Fire them. Fire them quickly. Terrorists delight in bringing misery to companies. I am a big fan of redemption, but fire them and make them reapply. Use the techniques in Chapter #6— Make the Interview Count—to reassess their commitment.

New Hires – New hires are the perfect candidates to become Unicorns. By looking for a new position, job searchers are already involved in a major change. New hires are anxious to show that they are the best possible hire. Make them prove it, ask them to read The Unicorn Path prior to starting their job and ask them if they are willing to participate in the 13-week Unicorn in

Training program. Unless you are hiring temporary workers, make every new hire work to be a future Unicorn.

Dealing with Failure

Always be searching for Unicorn candidates. Just agreeing to walk the Unicorn Path elevates performance. Unfortunately, some employees will decide that the required change is too much. The objective is to dominate the competition by having the most Unicorns.

Give your high-value craftsmen and key personnel room to leave The Unicorn Path. Change is hard. Thank them for trying, invite them to resume participation when/if they are more comfortable.

Be less patient with new hires. In most instances, a new hire who opts off The Unicorn Path should be terminated. New hires are your single biggest opportunity to build high-performing employees. Do not waste your valuable positions on people who do not want to improve.

Reflection Time

Loyalty is an important concept in business. There are many instances of companies rewarding employees for long service with loyalty, and there are many instances of employees staying with companies out of loyalty. To gain amazing success from a high-performance team, be loyal to *excellence rather than tenure.*

By walking The Unicorn Path, you are getting into the change business. The better your Company deals with change, the faster you will dominate the competition.

CHAPTER 5

Recruit Like You Sell

Compare how you sell with how you recruit. Most companies have detailed marketing plans, strong business development budgets, and great systems of sales accountability. Typically, the best and the brightest are focused on driving revenue. To build a team of Unicorns, you need to attack recruiting with the same passion, commitment, and ingenuity as business development. Visualize how your recruiting will improve if you use selling techniques to fill your Company with the best people.

Recruiting is the lead generation process of sales. The goal of lead generation is to get great meetings, and the goal of your recruiting process is to get great candidates to engage in your hiring process.

Here is a breakdown of the key components to Recruit Like You Sell:

<u>Love It</u> – I was watching a video of sales expert Grant Cardone. My favorite takeaway from his video was that you will never be great at sales if you do not love selling. Most businesses hate recruiting and view it as a disruptive inconvenience. If you do not love it, you will never be great. Fall in love. Make recruiting an important talking point in your Company and weave strong recruiting into your culture. Keep in mind that recruiting is the most critical path to your Company's success.

Be Fast – Speed to lead is critical in sales, and speed is crucial in recruiting. The best candidates will get the fastest offers. Being fast gives you first pick of the best talent. Being fast demonstrates to candidates that your Company is committed to excellence in your operations.

- Follow up on resumes and other talent leads as quickly as possible. Do not wait for a pile of resumes to accumulate. You would not wait for a bunch of leads to accumulate before you start selling.
- Perform your interview and related candidate due diligence as quickly as possible. Being fast does not mean being sloppy. Do what you need to do to become assured that you are making the right hire. Just do it as fast as you can.
- Make offers to the right candidates as quicky as possible.
- Track and report your recruiting speed.

Core Competency – If generating revenue is not a core competency, a company will not last long. I hear far too often that recruiting is not a company's core competency. If you believe that your success is based on the quality of people working in your Company, make recruiting a core competency. It is ok to get help, but if you want to be great, you need great people. Recruiting is the flywheel. Build your strategies around dominating in recruiting. Take advantage of the fact that most of your competition is uncomfortable with recruiting.

Be Special – Being like everyone else is like standing in line to get your fair share. The objective is to dominate the competition by stocking your Company with Unicorns. Look for every opportunity to stand out with a candidate. Assume that the second a prospective employee knows about your Company they are evaluating you.

Break down every stage of the interview from the initial scheduling to the final handshake and commit to showing every candidate that your Company is the best place for a great employee to work.

Continuously Recruit – Most companies have ongoing, consistent selling efforts. There is a constant need to grow and replenish revenue. Use the same practice for recruiting. By continuously recruiting, you will be developing rituals that will facilitate the process. Recruiting is typically inconvenient if it is not a ritual. Let your competition experience the inconvenience. Make committed recruiting part of your organization's routines. Set goals, hold your team accountable, and have someone on your team hold you accountable.

When you continuously recruit, there will be instances where you identify outstanding candidates without having any open positions. Treat this as a fantastic opportunity rather than a waste of time. Here are suggested options to deal with great candidates when there is no open position:

- Create a position – For an outstanding candidate, it may be worthwhile to create a new position. Use the investment vs expense evaluation process to determine if hiring the candidate would be an outstanding investment.
- Upgrade – If you have a position held by a tourist, consider upgrading that position with the new hire. It may sound cruel, but walking The Unicorn Path puts you on a mission to dominate the competition by building a high-performance team. Substituting a great candidate for a tourist coincides with that mission.
- Keep the candidate as a prospect – Tell the candidate that you greatly admire his or her attributes and that the candidate would be a great fit. Inform them that, regrettably,

there is no position currently available. Let them know that you are committed to building the best possible team and part of that process is to always be looking for great people. Apologize if they feel that they wasted their time. Ask them if it would be ok to follow up with them in the future when a position opens. Keep them on a drip contact campaign as you would with a sales prospect.

- Refer them to your network – Share leads with non-competing companies that embrace continuous recruiting. Identify companies that are committed to give as good as they get.

- Create a revenue resource – There will be companies that appreciate your process but are not interested in adopting continuous recruiting themselves. Consider charging referral fees for directing great candidates to other companies. Let other companies help you defray your recruiting cost.

- Help a customer – A great employee is the ultimate gift to a company. Helping a customer secure a great candidate will build fantastic relationships.

<u>Strive for Continuous Improvement</u> – It is often said that sales is a numbers game. It is indisputable that activity is the only mandatory aspect of sales; however, it is not just how much you do, it is how well you do it. The best salespeople are always looking to get better. The same tactics apply to recruiting. Constantly assess your processes and look to other organizations for best practices.

<u>Be Detached from the Outcome</u> – One of the most influential people in my professional life told me that the more he wanted a deal, the less attached he was to the outcome. It takes the guts of a cat burglar to create detachment from the outcome when you are faced with an enormous opportunity. However, it is amazing how

much better you sell when you do not project that you must have the deal. The same applies to recruiting. You are going to be sitting across from an incredible candidate. He or she will have an aura of excellence and a figurative glow. You start projecting how your profits will go up and your work hours will go down. This is the time when it is critical to stay relaxed and not project your desperate need.

Rejection is Not Failure – The selling process is packed with frustration. In sales, a prospect that absolutely needs your product or service will suddenly cease contact. Signed deals get cancelled because the incumbent comes back with a better offer. No matter how illogical prospects behave, a company will die if it does not keep selling. Recruiting has similar frustrations. People will commit to interviews and not show up. Great candidates will turn down your offers for irrational reasons. Candidates will say yes and change their minds. Even worse, they will say yes, not show up for their first day of work, and you will never hear from them again. This happens all the time. You can work your recruiting system to reduce defects in your process and enhance conversion, but you need to get comfortable with rejection, frustration, and irrational behavior.

Bad salespeople slow their activity when they hit a bad patch, but great salespeople get motivated and redouble their efforts. When you are recruiting, build the callouses that great salespeople have, and you will be miles ahead of your competition.

Recruiting Channels – The best sales lead generation plans have at least 4 channels to generate new prospects. I would like to encourage you to do the same with your recruiting efforts.

Each channel can be an aspect of Online, Social Media, Professional Recruiting, Networking, and other recruiting activities.

Online Resources such as Indeed or Zip Recruiter represent a critical channel that most companies utilize in their recruiting. Take the time to learn the nuances, track your results carefully, and know that even in an environment where everyone is doing it, you can be distinctly better.

Gain expertise in Social Media. Recruiting through LinkedIn and Facebook can be even more effective in recruiting than in sales. You can go shopping for the right candidates and reach out and send them a customized message to start the recruiting process.

<u>Professional Recruiters as a Channel</u> – Just because you need to develop recruiting as a core competency does not mean that you cannot get help. In sales, it is often a great practice to utilize agents or channel partners to carry part of the load. Great professional recruiters can be an incredible catalyst to building a talented team.

<u>Networking</u> – The best sales leads typically come from referrals and the best employees come from referrals as well. In networking, a Referral Partner is defined as someone who is focused on your target market without being a competitor. Great Referral partners start with your CPA, your banker, your lawyer, and your insurance agent. Create a list of targeted Referral Partners and create an action plan to systematically grow your network. Join groups with the emphasis on growing your Recruiting Referral Partner Network and meeting great candidates. Identify watering holes where your target candidates and Referral Partners hangout. Work to create a strong presence at the watering holes. Create understandings with your Referral Partners to include:

- I will appreciate and warmly welcome any referrals you send me. Do not worry about sending the "perfect" candidate. It is my job to determine if the person is a good fit, and I will never blame you if something goes wrong with one of your referrals.

- We are working to build a special culture at our Company. Do I have your permission to reject your referral if he or she is not a great fit?

Events - Make it easier for candidates to approach you. Develop events such as industry training, guest speakers, and happy hours to attract great candidates. Invite great prospects who are working for your competitors and give them a chance to see your high-performance culture.

Poaching – It is self-limiting thinking to believe that taking a high performer from a competitor is unethical or inappropriate. The mission is to dominate the competition by building a high-performance team. Your competitors are the best source of high performers. The commitment to The Unicorn Path demands that we use our most stringent efforts to employ great employees. If you do not have any problem taking their customers, use the same mindset to take their key people.

Often there is a concern that if you take one of theirs, they will take one of yours. When you build the right kind of high-performance environment, your Unicorns are not going anywhere.

You might be subject to a wage war, but you will find that money is not the biggest motivator for the highest performers.

Intel is critical – Build lists of great people that are working for your competitors. Ask suppliers and new hires for potential great hires. Be alert at industry events for prospects. Fill in the list with contact information. Use social media to learn about their interests. Create a campaign that focuses on culture, not money, and get the message out to your poaching list. Use your intel to go where your poaching prospects hang out. Emphasize confidentiality to let them know that they can speak with you without repercussions from their current employers. Inform them that you are interested but do not push them. Give them time to discover what makes you special. Finally, keep in mind that when you take a great employee from a competitor, you get a double benefit, both elevating your Unicorn count and diminishing your competitor's Unicorn Count.

Develop a Closing Strategy

Many bad salespeople lack a closing strategy. They just hope that the prospect says yes. Closing strategies are omitted from traditional recruiting practices as well. Typically, employers find someone they like, make an offer, and hope like the dickens that the candidate accepts. There is a better way!

Here is my recommended closing strategy:

- Let candidates know that it is ok to reject you. Let them know that at any stage of the process, if they find that your company is not the right fit, they are welcome to say no. No hard feelings. Wish them well.

- Always know where you stand. Each time you end a step in the recruiting process, get a status update from the prospect. I like to use the scale of 1 to 10 process. Ask the candidate on a scale of 1 to 10, with 10 being the highest, how interested are you in moving forward in your recruiting process? If the candidate gives an answer of 6 or below, it may be time to end the process. If they answer 6, 7, or 8, ask what it takes to get to a 10. Use that information to decide how to move forward. If you get a 9 or a 10, you know you are on the right track.

- Ask the candidate their decision-making process. Use this information to lock down a committed time for the final decision.

- Be ok with any outcome. You are on the path to greatness with or without the candidate.

The Unicorn Path creates an environment where you have a comprehensive, systematic, sales-oriented recruiting strategy. Recruiting is an incredible opportunity to dominate your competition. You focus on building a high-performance team and let your competition have the leftovers.

Reflection Time

Reflect on your past recruiting experiences. Consider stories you have heard from other business owners. Nearly all companies are getting failing grades. Rise up and kick butt.

CHAPTER 6

Make the Interview Count

Interviewing is typically uncomfortable, uninformative, and bland. To make your Company great, make the interview process great.

The Opportunity for Change

The core traits of a Unicorn are the willingness to improve personally, commitment to help their team improve, and the desire to make their company better. Improvement equals change, and most people are hesitant to change. The interview process is a major exception. Every candidate you speak with is in the process of a major change. They are considering a new job or even a new career.

As mentioned in Chapter #4 – The Unicorn Conversion Strategy, many of your existing employees will not be open to change. Capitalize on the interview process to populate your organization with people who want to be Unicorns. Adopt the mindset that you are not filling a spot, you are looking for a star. You are searching for the kind of employee who will make everybody at your Company better.

Make Your Purpose Known

Tell every, and especially every candidate you interview, that your Company believes:

- Great employees are worth more than great customers.
- We will dominate our competition by having great employees.
- To have great employees, we need to provide a great environment.
- We hire people who are great and people who want to be great.
- You cannot be great if you do not want to improve yourself, your team, and your Company.

Show Up with Great Energy

There have been too many instances of flat, emotionless interviews. You are searching for employees who want to walk your path. Give passion to get passion.

Set Ground Rules

Take the guessing out of the interview process by setting ground rules.

- Establish the length of the interview process. If you have planned 30 minutes, state that the interview will take 30 minutes. Typically, the interviewer has a fully scheduled day, and the best interviewees have tight schedules as well. The clarity of time enhances comfort for both parties. If the interview is trending long, work with the candidate to extend the interview time or set up a follow up interview.
- Restate your purpose. Do not worry about being tedious or repetitive. Your purpose is the guidewire for the entire process.

- Invite the candidate to hold you to the highest standards. Your Company is committed to being the best place for the best people. If the candidate observes any aspect of your operation that is not outstanding, invite them to bring it to your attention. Let them know that they are doing you a favor. To lower a candidate's filters, let them know that it is OK for them to play tough with you. You are looking for Unicorns who are passionate about improving your Company. Give recruits a chance to start helping you during the interview process.

- Ask for permission to ask the candidate difficult questions. Your objective is to get the best information to make your crucial hiring decision. Ask the right questions, no matter how tough they may be. By asking permission in advance and deploying a comforting tone, you will be far more likely to get a good reaction to a tough question.

- Install an interview ripcord. Ask permission to stop the interview if you determine that the candidate is not going to be a great fit. Give the candidate permission to stop the interview if he or she decides that your Company will not be a great fit. Agree that if either party pulls the ripcord, there will be no hard feelings.

- Discuss how the interview will end. It is crucial that you always know where you stand during the interview. Ask to spend the last 5 minutes of the interview talking about how to move forward. If you get to the end and it is a no go, let them know. If you get to the end and you are interested in the candidate, discuss the next steps and his or her decision-making process.

Ask Interview Questions with a Purpose

You are looking for high performers. Ask questions that will separate the stars from the pretenders. Be on the lookout for cues regarding improvement, teamwork, and happiness.

Stage 1 - Start with simple questions:

- What are you reading?
- Tell me about your experience at your last job?
- What is important to you in a job?

There is nothing original about these questions, but in the early stage, your questions should be designed to ease the candidate into a comfortable conversation.

Stage 2 – Drill down using these Questions:

These questions will get the candidate to open up and give you a better idea of who they are.

Follow-up questions to - what are you reading?

- How often do you read?
- How do you decide what to read?
- What else do you do to improve?

Follow-up questions to - tell me about your experience at your last job?

- Tell me about your immediate supervisor.
- Tell me about the owner/CEO.
- What was the company's mission statement?
- What was your favorite core value?

- How often did you receive raises and reviews?
- Did you ever have any disagreements with co-workers or leadership? If so, how did you handle the disagreements?
- Was there anything that you wish you would have said at your old job?
- Tell me about the extra things you did to help your former company succeed.

Follow up questions to - what is important to you in a job?

- What are your ideal hours?
- How do you like to receive feedback?
- What are the qualities of a great boss?
- When do you ask for help?
- How important is it to love your job?

Stage 3 - Move to the Challenge Round

Now it is time to get tough. This is the time when you challenge the candidate about the answers they provided in Stage 2, both what they said and what they did not say. You are looking for how the candidate reacts under pressure, you are looking for deeper engagement, and most importantly, you are looking to see if the candidate is interested in improving.

Here are some examples:

- Based on your responses, I have not heard anything that indicates that you are interested in improving. Is professional improvement important to you? Do you have any examples of initiatives you have taken to improve? Improvement is critical to our success. Would you be open to embracing the concept of continuously working to improve, *or should we pull the ripcord?*

- You did not mention loving your job as being important to you. We believe that you cannot be great at your job if you do not love your job. Can we talk about the importance of loving what you do, *or should we pull the ripcord?*

- You did not know your old company's core values or mission statement. Our mission and core values are critical to our high-performance culture. Would you be comfortable working in an environment where culture is key, or *should we pull the ripcord?*

Do not be afraid to suggest the ripcord. Your interview objective is to fill your Company up with high performers. When you suggest that you pull the ripcord, one of two things will happen. Either the conversation will improve and align to your purpose, or the interview will end. You should be ok with either of those outcomes.

Push for Commitment to The Unicorn Path

You are unlikely to find someone who has extraordinary answers to all your interview questions. The Challenger Step is designed to reveal the gap between an employee's standards and your requirements. You are looking for people that are passionate about improvement. The Challenger Step gets a candidate to commit to adhering to your standards. Saying it is good, writing it is better, and video is even better. If they will not commit to your high-performance values, give them the opportunity to work for your competition.

Reject with a Return Option

My father told me that there is no one as zealous as the converted. An interviewee that is unsuccessful may be an excellent candidate for conversion. When someone does poorly in an interview, politely reject them and give them a copy of The Unicorn Path (I apologize for the shameless plug). Let them know that if they read the book and are passionate about the content, they would be welcome to come back for another interview.

Evaluating Skills

In the absence of a trainee position, skills matter. Systematize your process by creating lists of the key duties and requirements. Create tests verified by experts. Fire a new hire fast if someone with misrepresented skills or poor character slips through the net.

Skills vs Attitude

During the interview process, you will encounter candidates that have outstanding skills, but no interest in walking the Unicorn Path. You are working to dominate your competition by building a high-performance team. The more Unicorns you have, the more success you will have. Providing a position to a new hire who is not interested in walking the Unicorn Path will set you back and send a message to your team that your commitment to high-performance needs improvement. Compromise equals two losers (the company and the employee). Scarcity is a big cause of compromise. Aggressively recruit so that you can aggressively interview.

The Pre-Hiring Agreement

Prior to shaking hands and getting the offer letter signed, make the following agreement with the future employee:

- We will win by having the best people. The best people are passionate about improving, helping teammates improve, and helping the Company improve.
- Our CEO has committed to focus on two areas – Making us the best place to work and providing business opportunities so that no high-performer will hit their ceiling.
- For us to meet our objective, we cannot waste a minute or a dollar on someone who does not share our values.
- None of us are perfect, and we have a deep commitment to our employees. We will fight to help you get back on track, but if it turns out that we cannot, do we have permission to let you go?

Most companies are not working on improving their interview process. They will continue to consider interviewing an uncomfortable and inconvenient process necessary to fill an open position. Interviewing is an opportunity to identify and hire the talent that will allow you to dominate your competition.

Reflection Time

You are looking to dominate the competition by having the best people. When the interview process gets you down, think about your competition interviews, and take the opportunity to be dramatically better.

CHAPTER 7

The Best Way to Build a Great Team is to Create a Great Environment

If your Company is not excellent, you cannot expect your employees to be excellent. By walking The Unicorn Path, you believe that great employees are better than great customers. Treat your employees better than your customers, and treat your customers fantastically.

Say It

Stand on top of the conference room table and shout that your Company is committed to being the best place to work for high performers. Say it often and say it passionately — this is in house advertising. You will win by capturing the hearts of high performers.

Ask

Avoid guessing. Ask Unicorns and Unicorns in Training what you can do to make your Company the best place to work. When you receive suggestions that are not viable, let your team know and thank them. Ask often. Unicorns are committed to helping their company improve. Let them help you to help them.

Do It

Be passionate in your execution. Move fast without being erratic. Strong responses to employee suggestions prove that you care.

Be Unique

You cannot be the best place to work if your environment is like everybody else's. Be distinctive. Feel free to steal ideas from other companies, but make sure your environment stands out.

Watch

Not every initiative you try will work. Carefully watch everything you do. Follow up with the team to get feedback. Monitoring what you are doing is the foundation for continuous improvement.

Get a Rep

Create a powerful buzz so that the business community knows that you are the premier place to work. When your employees tell their friends how happy they are, you get the best advertising. If you are not getting star recruits calling you from your competitors, you are not doing enough.

Money

Money is a mediocre motivator and a fantastic reward. The distinction is that money is a mid-tier way to get someone to be great, but a great vehicle to thank Unicorns for outstanding performance.

Pay your people well, but you do not have to pay the most to have the best.

Share the wealth. As you derive the incredible financial benefits from dominating your competition, carve out ample bonuses to thank your high performers for their incredible contributions.

Sustainability

Sustainability matters in a business environment too. Your goal is to pack your Company full of people who love their jobs. Working crazy hours for long periods of time is not sustainable. Happiness is a great reward, and it is hard to be happy if you do not have a personal or family life.

Set up rules for overtime for your team:

- Work overtime if it is time necessary to make customers happy.
- Limit recurring overtime situations by building a plan and getting help.
- Invest in yourself – feel free to spend extra time to get to the next level.
- Whenever possible, outperform do not outwork.

Career Clarity

A common Unicorn Path thread is that without clarity, there is no certainty; without certainty, there is anxiety. Clarity is an underappreciated component of a premier environment.

- Mission – make sure that everyone who receives a check from your Company memorizes your mission statement and understands his or her role in accomplishing the mission.

The mission is a company's purpose. Give your team the benefit of the power of your purpose.

- Core Values – Core values are a company's constitution, the rules that prevail above all else. The core values should be memorized and lived by everyone on the team.

- Goals – Goals are a proclamation of the most important commitments. By helping your team create the right goals, you will be helping them decide where to put their highest efforts.

- Performance Standards – Every team member should know exactly where they stand at all times, whether they are excelling or failing. Create a mechanism that lets your team know whether they are winning or losing.

- Compensation – There are too many instances of employees guessing the whats and whens of raises. Establish a program where employees understand both the amount and timing of their raises based on their performance.

- Promotions – This is another area where there is far too much uncertainty. Create a plan that shows each teammate the timing and requirements for their career path. Consider creating a projected 3-year org chart that allows your team to work toward potential opportunities.

Kind Words

It may seem like common sense but delivering kind words to employees is not common. Go out of your way to authentically say nice things. Celebrate wins. Thank people for their incredible effort. Console people when they stumble. Build it into your daily routine. Long after people have spent their Christmas bonuses, they will remember your encouraging words.

Food

Keep your refrigerator and your cabinets filled with snacks and drinks. Healthy is good, popular is better. Bring in catered meals regularly. Make everything free. Restock frequently. Food is comforting and stabilizing. Food is social; your team will bond over your free food. You will also get greater productivity as employees will have more energy and fewer reasons to leave the office.

Gifts

Give people gifts. Memorable is more important than expensive. Do not miss a birthday or work anniversary. Give gifts just because. Special bonus points if you get gifts for families as well.

There are shelves of books that state that givers get more than they give. Be a giving champion.

Ping Pong

I played a lot of ping pong as a kid. My eyes still light up every time I see a table, but overall, I am against people having fun at work by not working.

Rebrand Human Resources

Change the name of Human Resources to the Department of High Performance. Make attracting and retaining high performers the main focus of this department. The high energy skill set required to build a great team is far different than the compliant nature of human resources. I recognize that a company cannot function without payroll, benefits, or safety, but place your best resources in performance.

Reflection Time

The biggest benefit you can provide a high performer is to surround them with other high performers. It is much easier to go home with a smile on your face if your teammates are fully focused on helping you succeed. Great employees are an investment, not an expense. Invest the time and money to create an extraordinary environment for your Company. Most of your competitors have payrolls full of people who are not passionate about what they do. Whatever you spend on building a great place to work will be only a fraction of what is wasted by your competitors on the disengaged.

CHAPTER 8

High Performance Requires High Accountability

For high performers, accountability is recognition not punitive. Clarity is crucial in a high-performance environment. Accountability allows employees to know exactly where they stand. The best employees crave high accountability for the following reasons:

- Their goal is to be the best - Accountability can identify the best performers.

- They are always looking to improve – Accountability can identify and quantify areas of improvement.

- Team Building – much of the success for Unicorns will come from the support of teammates. Accountability will let Unicorns know where the rest of the team stands.

- Identify False Positives – nothing brings down the spirit of a team like a poor performer strutting around like a star. A strong system of accountability will let the whole company know who is winning and who is losing.

Define High Performance

Unicorns need to have a clear picture of your Company's performance standards. It is easier to win the performance game when Unicorns know the rules. Here are suggestions for your Company's performance standards:

The Unicorn Core – Measure commitment to self-improvement, team improvement and Company improvement.

Your Company's Core Values – Measure how well each employee lives each of your core values.

Goal Status – Track the status for 30 and 90-day goals.

The Unicorn Core and Company Core Values measure attitude. Goal status aligns with job performance and focuses on the most important tasks.

Measure High Performance

Performance measurement is an important component of The Unicorn Path. Quantifying accountability drives high performance. I like to use a scale of 1 to 10 to score attitude and jobs measurements. Use 10 as the highest score and 1 as the lowest. There is a risk of subjectivity with a ten scale. You can reduce this risk with clearly defined standards for each number and using consistent evaluators.

Add the performance measurements to your Company's scoreboard system. Use the results to celebrate wins and to help pull stragglers up.

Performance Feedback

High-frequency feedback equals high performance. Performance evaluations can be uncomfortable for both the giver and the receiver. Many people do not feel comfortable with confrontation of any type. It takes commitment and resolve to work with your team to overcome the discomfort of evaluations. A core foundation of a Unicorn is to continuously improve. The best way to continuously improve is to get constant feedback, both good and bad. Make the message as uplifting as possible but stick with the facts. If you want to build a great team, give them great feedback frequently:

<u>Daily</u> – Critical feedback is the foundation of improvement. If someone in your Company sees an issue, it is his or her duty to point out the problem to a Unicorn. Using the techniques discussed in Unicorn Principle #9 – Conflict is the Ultimate Competitive Advantage, teach your high performers to deliver the ongoing tough truth in an effective manner.

<u>Weekly</u> – Weekly employee evaluations provide the gift of clarity. To be sustainable, the weekly evaluation process needs to take no more than 5 minutes. The objective of the 5-minute meeting is to let each employee know where they stand:

- Focus on Unicorn core, Company core values, and goal status.
- Have the employee being reviewed self-score using the 1 though 10 scale.
- The supervisor will help refine/edit the self-score.
- Make notes of parking lot issues that arise.
- Work to make it the same day and time each week.
- Strive to make every meeting. Use phone calls or video conferencing when you cannot meet in person.

- You cannot solve a serious problem during a 5-minute meeting. If you have a major issue, schedule an additional session.

Monthly

Allocate one hour for each monthly review. Focus on the progress documented during the weekly review. Develop new 30-day goals. Discuss the employees career path. Review their Unicorn workbook.

Quarterly

Allocate 2 to 3 hours for a quarterly review.

- Celebrate the employee's achievements during the past quarter.
- Review The Unicorn Core – What did the employee do to improve? What did the employee do to make others better? What did the employee do to make your Company better?
- Update the 30 and 90-day goals. Make sure that the goals are aligned with your Company's goals and mission.
- Discuss what worked and what did not work.
- Go over every page of the employee's Unicorn Principles Workbook (The Workbook is discussed further in Section 2 and is available by emailing info@UnicornPath.com) Pick out key items and set improvement goals.
- Review the employee's career path for the next 12 months, focusing on tasks, position, and compensation. Discuss what needs to happen to get to the next level.

Your evaluation time is valuable. If an employee is struggling, either terminate them or fix them before sitting down with them for a 3-hour meeting.

Annual

Make the annual review a companywide event.

- Celebrate the wins enthusiastically.
- Provide everyone with updated Company goals and strategies.
- Make sure that every employee has a clear understanding of his or her role in your Company's mission.

Win the Battle for a New Employee's Soul

Accountability is crucial during a new employee's first 90 days (13 weeks). New employees are brimming with enthusiasm and ambition. If a new employee does not have adequate clarity and accountability during the first 90 days, enthusiasm will turn into the dead stare of disengagement. The following are suggestions to enhance accountability during the first 90 days:

- Create a 13-week work plan that provides a map of the employee's responsibilities and performance requirements for each workday.
- Assign a fellow Unicorn Path employee as a mentor. When the new employee has a question or concern, they will initially go to the assigned mentor.
- The employee's supervisor should perform the 5-minute evaluation every workday.
- Periodically (at least weekly) quiz the employee on your Company's mission statement and core values.
- Take the time to help a new employee get better.
- Fire a new employee the second you determine that the new employee is not committed to walking The Unicorn Path.

Create a Firing System

Firing someone, even a terrorist, can be a stressful process. Doubt creeps in. Did you do enough to help the employee be successful? From the employee's perspective, I have experienced countless instances where an extremely poor performer was shocked by their termination. Work to strip subjectivity out of the termination process. By effectively executing a strong employee review system, every employee should know exactly where they stand. Every employee should have a development plan. If an employee stumbles in their attitude or performance, help them get them back on the path. If they cannot get back on track, fire them.

I advocate using Green, Yellow, and Red employee status levels:

Green – The employee is on track on all major issues. Focus should be based on getting to the next level and dialing in small issues.

Yellow – The employee is having frequent relatively minor issues with his or her performance. Identify the improvement issues and develop a plan to get the employee back on track. Get them the help that they need. Give them 90 days to get back to green. Terminate the employee if they do not get back on track within the allotted time.

Red – The employee is having serious problems with attitude and/or performance. Focus on the seriousness of the situation. Communicate that the employee will be terminated within a week unless major progress is made on the problems.

As bad as a termination can be for the employee, your Company also loses the time and money invested in the terminated employee's development. Poor performers drag down the entire team. It is critical to your High-Performance mission to clear out employees that are not interested or capable of becoming valuable members of your high-performance team.

Scoreboards

Scoreboards are a fantastic way to advertise accountability to your Company's employees. Your Company's scoreboard can be as simple as a white board or as intricate as a network of video screens. The objective of a scoreboard is to report accountability on an ongoing basis. Metrics, also referred to as Key Performance Indicators (KPIs), are great ways to quantify performance. Here are some suggestions for your Company's scoreboard:

- Daily Winning or Losing - Look for metrics that express your success daily. Look for the most important daily number. In many instances, the number can be estimated daily profitability. Also, look for the daily critical number for each employee and incorporate each employee's score into your scoreboard.

- Goals – Have the scoreboard reflect where your Company and your employees stand on their goals. Indicate where goals are trending poorly. Advertise to your team for help in getting back on track.

- Employee Performance – You can quantify employee performance. Advertise the number of Unicorns you have. Post the Unicorn Workbook scores. Post great employee achievements.

- Gamification - Gamification is the application of elements of game playing to business activities. Use gamification to create contests and milestones.

There is more on scoreboards in Unicorn Principle #16 Keep Score to get more.

Reflection TIme

Your goal is to dominate the competition by having a dramatically better team. Most of your competition is not taking the time to provide effective ongoing accountability. You cannot win the game if you do not know the score.

CHAPTER 9

Build a Factory

You will never have a high-performance team if your Company does not build high performers. Poaching great employees from other Companies is a great strategy, but it is unlikely that you will be able to assemble enough poached employees to create a high-performance team.

Desire

Desire matters. Most companies are not even thinking about building a strong employee development program. Commitment and great strategies are born from great passion.

Commitment

Development = Improvement = Change

With change comes discomfort. Your best employees may see an employee development program as unnecessary or a threat. Commitment is the strongest way to get through change. The more Unicorns you develop the better your Company. Financial prosperity and happiness abounds in a Unicorn high performance environment.

Employee development is a cornerstone of building a high-performance team. Like all major initiatives there will be setbacks. Use a strong resolve to fight through setbacks. Know that building a great team will lead to competitive dominance.

It Takes a System

Often leaders point to great performers and wish that they had more of them. In the absence of a high-performance employee development system, each employee must figure out the path to success for themselves. The Unicorn Path is a system of employee performance that is teachable and duplicable.

- The Unicorn Principles –The Unicorn Principles (see Section II) form a system of employee high-performance. Use The Unicorn Principles as the foundation of your factory. The more employees who live The Unicorn Principles, the more success your Company will experience.
- Next Level EQ (emotional intelligence) – Build upon The Unicorn Principles to develop programs that focus on emotional intelligence (EQ). Create programs that enhance communication and interpersonal skills. Use books and internet resources for individual programs. Look to outside speakers and other resources to help improve your team's overall EQ.
- Job Skills – Do everything you can to accelerate job skill knowledge. Create training programs, authorize overtime, assign mentors. The faster people who live the Unicorn Principles master their job skills, the faster you win.

Reflection Time

Building a high-performance employee development factory will be a significant investment. Carefully plan your investments, set goals for expected returns from your factory investment. Adjust and persevere. Unicorns will bring you incredible prosperity, happiness, and the security of knowing that you are dominant in your marketplace.

SECTION II
THE UNICORN PRINCIPLES

THE UNICORN PRINCIPLES

An Introduction

The previous section of this book focused on providing companies with the tools to create an environment that will lead to competitive dominance.

This section – The Unicorn Principles – is geared towards individual high performance.

The essential core of a Unicorns is:

- Continuous improvement,
- Working to make others better
- A passion to contribute to a Company's success.

This section weaves this core with the 17 Unicorn Principles to create a powerful employee high performance operating system.

PRINCIPLE 1

Walk the Path of Excellence (The Unicorn Path)

> *"The will to win, the desire to succeed, the urge to reach your full potential these are the keys that will unlock the door to personal excellence."*
> – CONFUCIUS

ex·cel·lence: the quality of being outstanding or extremely good.

What the Disengaged Does:

- They focus on just getting by – doing what it takes to get through the day.
- They are highly resistant to change/improvement.
- They value tenure rather than ability.

It is easy for life to get in the way and knock you off The Unicorn Path. You cannot be excellent every minute of every day. When the hardships and distractions of life knock you off the path, fight to get back. Remember that your objective is to become a high performer in the business world, and striving for excellence on The Unicorn Path is the way to get there.

The pursuit of excellence in the workplace is frustratingly rare. The 70% of the workforce that are disengaged have no interest in everyday excellence. By simply striving to be excellent in everything you do, you will put yourself ahead of all the disengaged in the most important category – ATTITUDE.

Excellence does not have to take more time. It does not have to cost more money. It is about the desire to wake up each day striving to be better.

You Are Your Own Best Investment

It is human nature to minimize expenses and optimize investments. For the right investment, people will sell everything they own. Become your own best investment. Passionately invest in professional development and in mastering your job skills. It does not have to cost a lot of money, but you will need to invest committed time to become a Unicorn. Go all in to becoming the best you.

Here are the payoffs:

- You will love what you do.
- The people that you work with and for will love you.
- You will make dramatically more money over the course of your career
- You will have the best kind of job security, the security that comes from being extremely valuable.
- Your value will be easily recognized in the business world, which will give you the flexibility to find rewarding employment elsewhere should you choose.

- The skills that you develop at work will translate to a better personal life in the forms of more personal time, less anxiety, and more tranquility.

Perfection is the Enemy of Excellence

The most successful people do not make fewer mistakes. They recover from their mistakes faster.

Mistakes are inevitable. Even the most cautious frequently make mistakes (they may be reluctant to admit it). People who fear making mistakes almost always work at a slow pace. You cannot be great if you cannot be prolific. Work hard, be conscientious, and know that mistakes are the necessary byproduct of excellence.

Care more, worry less, and recover faster.

Surround Yourself with People who are Also Interested in Improving

Jim Rohn said, "You are the sum of the 5 people that you spend the most time with." The more time you spend with successful people, the more successful you will be. You will pick up their habits, you will share ideas, and you will make each other better.

To make a major breakthrough, find a mentor, especially a mentor who is currently outside your current circle of familiarity. When you learn from someone outside your circle, you will gain different perspectives, and you will gain access to a new network of resources.

When searching for a mentor, do not take the easy route. Go searching for big game. Your target is someone who will help you walk the path of excellence. The better your mentor, the better your progress. Be persistent, be aggressive, and be creative in your search for a mentor. Ask your employer for suggestions. Ask your friends and networks for suggestions. Research Linked In and other internet sites to find potential mentors. Make a list of successful people that you would like to meet and plan to meet them. The only barrier to getting a meeting with a prospective mentor is your commitment to getting that meeting.

Persistence is richly rewarded in life. Do not let the fear of rejection or any other anxiety get in the way of your pursuit of getting a mentor. It will surprise you how many accomplished professionals are happy to help others. If it turns out that he or she does not want to help you, no harm done. Pick yourself up, recover from the rejection, dust yourself off, and go find someone else.

Learn to move on. If a mentor or a group does not support your purpose, find a new one. Leave politely but leave. Treat your time with great value.

Join groups that fit in with your path. If you are not a good speaker, join the Toastmasters. Look for associations and Linked In groups in your quest for improvement. Work to connect with members of groups knowing that the more time you spend with great people, the better you will become.

Create Improvement Goals

Goals are the key for the most effective people to accomplish their most important tasks.

Great goals are broken down into weekly, monthly, and yearly milestones. Share your goals, post your goals, and get help to help to keep you on track.

Goals are crucial in dealing with day-to-day obstacles that get in the way of your progress. Stephen Covey referred to the things that get in between you and your most important things as the whirlwind. The reality of day-to-day life is going to smack you off your path of excellence. The whirlwind is a powerful adversary to your success, and the key to beating back the whirlwind is strong goal orientation.

Goals are documented commitments, and as such, will be covered in far more detail in Principle #3 – What You Commit to Gets Done.

Build a Plan with Your Employer

Do not make the mistake of relying on your employer to provide them with a method for improvement. Do not wait for your Company to make you great. Most companies do not excel at employee development. Take the initiative to build a high-performance culture in your Company

You are in charge of your plan. Walking the path of career excellence is hard (if it were not, everybody would be doing it). Remember that everything is better with the right kind of help, and your Company is in a position to give you the best kind of help. Share your plan with your employer, ask them for feedback, help, and oversite. The better you are, the better it is for your Company.

If you hit a roadblock with your employer, do not get discouraged and do not give up. Reassess your plan, evaluate why you hit the roadblock, and persist until you get what you want.

Create an Accountability Group

A few years ago, I attended a speech by an author who wrote a book on the successful characteristics of billionaires. One of my favorite takeaways from the seminar was a story about an accountability group that met for breakfast every Tuesday for more than 20 years, and 2 of the members became billionaires.

An accountability group is a gathering of people who share their goals and support each other in reaching them. Create a group of 3 to 8 people with complementary career objectives. Set up recurring meetings and create an environment where your group makes each member better. Research best Accountability Group practices on the internet and use your network to correspond with other Accountability Groups to share best practices. A strong accountability group will drive you to develop effective goals, read more books, and share thoughts and ideas that help you deal with obstacles as they emerge. Let it be your autobahn for self-improvement.

What are You Reading?

I frequently ask this question during interviews, and I rarely get a good answer. When I get a poor response, I know that the interviewee is not likely to be committed to continuous improvement. Reading is an incredible way to build your skills. Determine what you need to be successful, and start reading books in those genres. Ask people that you admire what they are reading. Start book clubs to discuss. Use Audible or other audiobook tools to learn while you are driving.

You cannot be excellent without improvement, and reading is one of the best ways to improve.

Team Up with Your Peers

Yes, I am suggesting that you work with what many would consider to be the competition — co-workers who are vying for the same career path and resources as you are. This is a counterintuitive idea, but there are unlimited opportunities for people committed to excellence who are walking The Unicorn Path. Take the help to get to the top. Work to make others better. There is plenty of room for success. The more Unicorns, the better.

I believe that the single most powerful influence on change/improvement are peer groups. No one has more influence on your performance than the person working right next to you.

Build a Scoreboard

When we were growing up, most of us would not even consider playing a game if we did not keep score. Now that we are working instead of playing, most of us do not think about keeping score. Seize on the motivation that scoreboards once provided us. Create metrics associated with your key goals. Track these metrics and report them on a scoreboard. Your scoreboard can be as simple as post-it notes or a section of a white board. Fancy does not matter; the key is for you to be able to visualize your progress on the path.

Tracking metrics via a scoreboard will be covered in depth in Principle #16 – Keep Score to Get More.

Red Team

A **red team** is a group that challenges an organization to improve its effectiveness by assuming an adversarial role or point of view. Red Teams are often used to assess the effectiveness of battle plans for the military. Most people are hesitant to invite criticism. You will prosper from hearing what you might be doing wrong. Pick people:

- Who you respect
- Who understand and support your career path

- Who are willing to deliver tough feedback in a constructive way

Get Frequent Feedback

I visit a lot of companies that cannot even remember the last time they performed employee evaluations. Since knowledge is power, always knowing where you stand at your job is incredibly powerful.

Ask your employer for a Frequent Feedback Program. Work to set up a weekly evaluation. Keep it short, 5 minutes or less (the longer the meeting, the less sustainable the process). Give your employer permission to play tough with you but ask that they deliver the feedback in a constructive manner. You can obtain a template of what I use by e-mailing info@UnicornPath.com and requesting the 5-minute evaluation form.

Spend the last minute of the session developing a plan to address any issues.

The Value of Scarcity

The Unicorn Principles are designed to provide you with an employee performance operating system. As a Unicorn, you will become a highly valued member of the business community. Most believe that excellence is valuable in the workplace, but almost no one walks a path of excellence at their job. Walk the path, live the Principles, and rise above others in the workplace.

PRINCIPLE 2

Purpose is a Superpower

| *"He who has a why to live can bear almost any how"*
– FRIEDRICH NIETZSCHE

pur·pose: the reason for which something is done or created or for which something exists.

What the Disengaged Does:

- They do not have a powerful purpose for their career
- They are not connected to their Company's vision
- They are not rowing in the same direction as their Company

Get a Big Why

Everyone can master The Unicorn Principles. It is purely a matter of your commitment and desire. A strong purpose is the ultimate driver of commitment and desire. The Unicorn Principles do not require completion of quadratic equations, lifting of heavy objects, or challenging hikes. To successfully master The Unicorn Principles, you will need to:

- Embrace change
- Dramatically alter your communication style
- Destroy your comfort zones
- Disrupt your rituals and routines

On the surface it does not seem bad, but your brain's operating system is designed to resist all these changes. If you can fight through the resistance, you will change your life, but *you have no prayer of breaking through without a strong purpose.*

Superpower

Being able to fly is a superpower. X-Ray vision is a well-acknowledged superpower, and incredible strength or speed would come in handy. I submit to you that a strong purpose is right up there on the superpower list.

In support of my assertion, let us start with Nietzsche's quote – *"with the right purpose you can endure almost any how."* The most powerful example that I am aware of came from Viktor Frankl's book, "Man's Search for Meaning." In his book, Frankl describes his experiences as a prisoner in Nazi Concentration camps during World War II. He describes the evilest acts of human cruelty and the unimaginable hardships he endured. He makes a very convincing case that the power of purpose was the only reason that he was one of the small fraction of survivors. His desire to be reunited with his wife and his passion to complete his work in logotherapy gave him the power to survive the most challenging circumstances imaginable.

Ant and Elephant

In his book, "The Ant and the Elephant," author Vince Poscente discusses the dynamic between our conscious and subconscious minds. He describes the conscious mind as having the size and power of an ant, while the subconscious mind has the size and power of an elephant. When you aspire to make major changes in your operating system, you go to battle with your subconscious mind, the elephant. Our subconscious mind tries to protect us against the unfamiliar.

Our conscious minds respond to intellectual stimulus (hows and whats), while our subconscious minds respond to emotional and visual stimulus (why's). We spend most of our lives training the ant by reading and learning, but most of us let the elephant run free. The Unicorn Principles is packed full of techniques to help train your elephant, but it starts with a powerful why.

Simon Sinek

Simon Sinek's incredible success is based on the word Why. In his bestselling book, "Start with the Why," Sinek makes a great case that people do not care about how or what you are doing, they care about why you are doing it. He uses compelling examples of how Steve Jobs, Martin Luther King Jr., and the Wright Brothers used the power of why to spread incredible messages. Check out Simon Sinek's Ted Talk to learn more about the power of why.

Vision Board

A Vision Board is a visualization tool that refers to a board of any sort used to build a collage of words and pictures to represent your goals and dreams.

When I first heard of vision boards, I thought it was a bunch of hippie nonsense. Then I started to hear stories from successful people I respected. The subconscious mind responds to images. Vision boards speak directly to the elephant! As part of starting the Unicorn journey, I encourage you to create your own vision board to reflect how your life will look once you have become a high-performing Unicorn. Cut out pictures from magazines or use the power of the internet to select meaningful images of how your deeply enhanced success will influence you, your spouse, your children, your house, your car, your travel, and your wellbeing. Get those images mounted on cardboard or poster board and put your board at a place where you will see it often. My vision board is my screen saver. As a result, I look at my vision board at least 10 times daily. Every time you need a dose of motivation or assurance, get your eyes on your board.

Examples of Purposes

Strive to individualize your purpose, to make it extra meaningful for you personally. Make your purpose about more than money. Here are some examples:

- I want to be the best.
- I want to be special, and I want to work for a company that recognizes special performers
- I want to be a great performer in a great company.
- Happiness matters. I want to be great at a job that I love.

Mission & Vision

A company's mission is its purpose, and a company's vision is its future purpose. Most companies do not emphasize their mission and vision, and accordingly, most employees do not have any connection with their Company's purpose.

- For optimum effectiveness, work to align your purpose with your Company's mission.
- If your Company's mission statement is not inspiring, help them improve it.

- Encourage your co-workers to align with your Company's mission statement and vision. It is like getting everyone in a boat to row in the same direction.

The Value of Scarcity

Your objective is to become an extremely valuable member of a high-performance team. If you want to stand out from the rest, utilize the superpower of purpose.

PRINCIPLE 3

What You Commit to Gets Done

> *"Motivation is what gets you started. Commitment is what keeps you going."*
> – JIM ROHN

com·mit·ment: the state or quality of being dedicated to a cause, activity, etc.

What the Disengaged Does:

- They give up when things get tough
- Their productivity is based on short term needs and demands
- They take the easy route

What you Commit to Gets Done

Excluding activities that defy the rules of physics, you can accomplish anything with the right commitment and the right actions. If you are late to a meeting, it is because you were not committed to being on time. If you do not complete a project, it is because you were not committed to completing the project.

A lack of commitment does not mean you are a bad person, it typically means that you were committed to something else. You might be late to a meeting because you were committed to spending a couple more minutes finishing an important e-mail to a client.

Commitment Hesitancy

Commitment is critical to any change of routine or any activity that threatens your mental status quo. Our brain is geared to treat change with skepticism and hesitancy. Additional caution comes from failure or the chance of failure.

One of the most aggressive remedies to commitment hesitancy was when the Spanish Conquistador, Hernan Cortes, ordered his boats burned when he and 600 men arrived in Mexico in 1519. They had no choice but to go forward and succeed. There was no retreat.

I suspect that most of you will not need to burn anything to fulfill your commitments, but you will need help to avoid the powerful pull of hesitancy and procrastination. Burn your mental boats. Endure temporary hardships of frustrating change for the bounty that comes from being able to commit to excellence.

Focus

Your ability to successfully accomplish your most important activities will be your key to success. The problem is that there is intense competition from everything else. Daily tasks can range from running household chores to multimillion-dollar presentations. Even the least significant tasks cry out for your attention. If you are not clear with your task commitments, even the smallest of problems can crush your ability to focus on the most important activities.

Goals are a Listing of Your Commitments

Goals are a list of your commitments. In the absence of clear, powerful goals, you lose a great deal of control over influencing your fortunes. Doing your best is not a strategy. Some people can be successful without commitment and goals. In the Beverly Hillbillies, Jed Clampett was hunting for rabbits when he found oil. People without goals have been, and will continue to be, successful. Unfortunately, the majority of the goal-less get far less than the relentlessly focused.

SMART Goals

A popular tool used in goal development is the acronym SMART. It is hard to argue with the practicality of SMART goals. Here is a listing by letter with **Unicorn amendments**:

Specific – a clear, understandable goal has a much better option for success. **The most critical component of a specific goal is that is should clearly coincide with your purpose. Fight to avoid goals that do not coincide with your purpose.**

Measurable – does the goal provide you with an opportunity to assess whether you are winning or losing? I have seen many initial goals that stated, I want to be a better listener or be a better leader. Your goal needs to be measurable so that **you know whether you are winning or losing on a daily basis.**

Attainable – do you have a plan, and does your company have the realistic resources to allow you to accomplish the goal? **There can be a wrong time for the right goal.**

Realistic – do you have a likely chance of accomplishing your goal? Under promising and over-delivering is a common way to address issues with goal accomplishment success. I believe that "sandbagging" is extremely unproductive. If your objective is to crush every goal and stay out of trouble, then under promise and over-deliver. However, if your objectives coincide with being a high-performing employee, set aggressive goals.

Timely – each goal should have time frames. The most effective goal accomplishment calls for granular daily activity. For optimal effectiveness, set daily, weekly, 90-day, 1-year and 5-year goals.

UNICORN Additions to SMART:

- Be relentless – You are doing this to change your life and to dramatically add value to your career. Fight! Do not surrender! When you get knocked down (and you will), get back up.
- Make sure that your work goals and purpose coincide with your Company's management. In a Covey survey, half of all employees are not connected with their Company's purpose. Collaborate with leadership to make sure that your goals are giving you optimal work effectiveness.
- Learn to Fail – This is overlap, as we have a whole principle on this, but your best way to improve is to rid yourself of the fear of failure when you are building great goals. Forgive yourself. You are on a journey to accomplish more than you could ever imagine. There will be many instances where you reach for the stars and hit the moon.
- Put Your Goals in Writing –There is a deeper mental connection when you handwrite your goals. Feel free to use

computer-generated techniques to publicize your goals but handwrite when possible, to get a tighter connection.

- Frequency is a key influencer - The more often commitment is expressed, the stronger it becomes. Review your goals at least once a week and preferably every day. Stay connected with your goals.

- Advertise your goals – Let everyone you work with learn your goals. You will get enhanced accountability, and your goal visibility will provide many opportunities for your team to contribute to your success.

- Continuously report your status – The "Expectation Gap" is a leading cause of frustration in business. Let your team, especially leadership, know how you are doing on your goals. If you are falling behind, ask for advice as to how to move forward. If necessary, consider postponing or removing goals.

- Get Help – A goal means that you have committed to an outcome or result. It does not mean that you must be the only one to work on the project. An accountability group or an accountability partner can be extremely valuable. You are walking a challenging path. Build a team to help you keep on the path, and most importantly, help you get back on the path when you fall off.

- Evaluate Your Goal Related Actions – Continuously review your actions to evaluate whether your actions coincide with your goals. If your actions are not aligned with your goals, work to change your actions

- Understand Priorities – Have clear rules on your priorities. For instance, how do you react to family issues, especially family emergencies?

- Time management – Your time is crucial, and the better you manage your time, the more successful you will be. **Stay out of Sidetrack City.** Avoid interruptions by blocking out times when you are not available (unless there is an emergency), limit meeting times by using crisp agendas, keep conversations from drifting off-topic.

- Say "No" More often – Most of us want to be nice. Saying yes is a big part of being perceived as nice. Set expectations in advance so that the requester understands why you are saying no.

- Stop Doing – Keep a notebook handy and make a list of things that you currently do that do not coincide with your purpose and goals. Share your list with teammates and Company leadership to help build a path away from these activities.

- Continuously evaluate your goals – Your goals are subject to change. There will be several instances when you select the wrong goal, or your goal needs modification. Do not wimp out and change a goal because it is hard. Feel free to change goals to enhance your performance.

The Value of Scarcity

Commitment is a skill that can be developed. The better your commitment, the better your value in the workplace. The better your commitment skills, the better person you will be. Treat it like a muscle and build your commitment.

PRINCIPLE 4

You Can Change, or You Can Stay the Same

"Growth is painful. Change is painful. But nothing is as painful as staying stuck where you do not belong."
– N.R. NARAYANA MURTHY

Change: make or become different.

What the Disengaged Does:

- They fear change
- They rationalize reasons to resist
- They actively and passively attack the elements of change
- They discourage change in others

Know What You Are Up Against

You are on a path to become a remarkable and distinctively valuable contributor to your Company's success. There is no lottery to win these skills, there is no magic pill that will suddenly make you exceptional, and there is not an app on your phone that will instantly make you great. To be exceptional, you need to have a strong plan and a passion for constantly getting better.

Regardless of where you are today, continuous improvement is critical to sustain success. Fall in love with getting better. Once you get comfortable with constant improvement, the anxiety of change will be replaced with satisfaction and exhilaration.

When I ask who is interested in improvement to a room full of people, every hand shoots up. When I ask who wants to change, there is a lot of hesitancy. Improvement = Change, improvement is just a softer word. Nothing in this book works without change. Change does not happen without you being mentally prepared. It takes work to free yourself from a lifetime of programming your subconscious. Logically, there are few reasons to resist change's positive synonym improvement. In the absence of incredible success or retirement, why would a person resist positive change? Yet, the common bond of the 70% disengaged is resistance to meaningful improvement.

This book provides a number of tools to overcome resistance to change. Jump on the path. Make change a habit and enjoy life as a high performer.

Your Comfort Zone is Not Your Friend

A comfort zone is a state of psychological familiarity. The comfort zone is an area of low stress and low anxiety. As children, we grow up with incredible dreams of living a wonderful life founded on purpose, accomplishment, and success. Most do not get close to accomplishing these dreams. There are lots of causes, but a major reason is that familiarity is not your friend. By choosing familiarity over change, you choose your comfort zone over improvement. Your comfort zone is not your friend. Think of it as a vacuum that is sucking the dreams out of your soul.

Feeling comfortable is important. We develop routines and habits to keep us in our comfort zones. I am a big fan of comfort, but real comfort is not rooted in familiarity. Minimalizing stress and anxiety is valuable; but, how comfortable can you be as a commodity in the workplace? Consider how much stress and anxiety is caused by being mediocre in the workplace. The Unicorn Path is to achieve comfort and freedom from stress and anxiety by being excellent. By improving who we are. By improving so much that we get more while experiencing less stress.

Familiarity keeps whispering, "stay on the comfort zone couch with me." This is a safe place. When you do not change, when you sit on the comfort zone couch, you forgo a huge chunk of what could be your life in exchange for the numbness of familiarity.

I am not asking you to throw away your comfort zone. I am asking you to embrace the Unicorn Principles to make a deliberate, committed, bloodless coup against familiarity/status quo and re-orient your mental operating system so that you find comfort in improvement and excellence.

"A problem is only a problem when viewed as a problem. All change is hard at first, messy in the middle, and gorgeous at the end."
– ROBIN SHARMA

Fear of Failure - Quiet Desperation

I often reflect on Thoreau's message that "the mass of men (and women) lead lives of quiet desperation." Thoreau asserts that the greed to want more luxurious and unnecessary things in life is the cause of all the anxiety and the primary cause of quiet desperation. Today, it is referred to as getting caught in the rat race. Greed and lust for material things can be extremely destructive. I believe that a huge contributor to desperation is the gap between what you want and what you have. The Unicorn Principles are excellence-driven, not greed-driven.

While the lust for more is a problem, I submit that the true cause of "quiet desperation" is too many failed trips outside our comfort zone. It is our fear of failure and the inability to recover that causes us to retreat from our dreams. I have heard many stories of people not interested in falling in love because they do not want to get hurt again, or I'm happy at this position because I can't handle the stress of looking for something else. Life is too short to have that inner sense of despair that lives in too many of us. Our freedom from despair lies from learning to be more rather than striving to scale back.

The Japanese have institutionalized quiet desperation. Japanese executives who have reached a dead zone in their careers are often called the "window tribe." They are the abandoned souls of corporate Japan. They do little but stare aimlessly out their office window. They have grown to the ubiquitous point where a Forbes article refers to them as Japan's Window Zombies. They are the convergence of unfulfilled accomplishment and Japan's tradition of not terminating workers. They are the epitome of the desperate soul that proliferates in a subtler manner in the United States.

People Who Cannot Change Aren't Bad

People who cannot change are normal. They are ordinary. It does not mean that they are bad people. It means they never had the means to break out of that cocoon that holds back our dreams. They live on auto-pilot. They go to work, get married, have kids, stay busy, buy things, and get along. They forget their dreams. They choose the safety of a static life over the potential failure of striving for their dreams.

We are our own worst enemy. Our instinctual mental operating system is designed to keep us safe. It worked great when changing caves might mean moving in with a sabretooth tiger, but the safety of consistency ultimately becomes a trap as the unwillingness to improve turns good people into commodities. It is rare when the business community treats commodities with value.

What Motivates Change

The motivation of change must be greater than the motivation to stay the same. Your operating system will not let you off your "comfort couch" easily. It will pull and tug you until you either break away or surrender. Meaningful change only comes with a strong purpose.

If you are not getting enough, attack your comfort zone and challenge the habits and routines that are holding you back.

Get angry, get frustrated, gather yourself, get a purpose, get committed, and make yourself a star.

I am not afraid to get hokey and suggest that every letter in the word change is also contained in the word challenge. Rise to the challenge.

The great thing is that if you can break through the pain and resistance of change, you can do anything.

When you embrace change, success and fulfillment will embrace you back.

The Benefits of Change - MMA is My Favorite Example

MMA stands for mixed martial arts. I have never participated in MMA in any manner. I am not a big fan of MMA, but I am a huge fan of the best fighter's commitment to improve. MMA fighters without sufficient commitment to excel suffer incredible penalties. MMA fighters with a premier path towards excellence receive incredible financial rewards and more importantly, they receive the ratification that they are premier in their field.

Even a middle-of-the-pack MMA professional fighter can defeat the most formidable untrained brawler.

Unlike MMA, the pain of defeat in someone's business career is not as abrupt and obvious. Not being as good rarely yields any blood or bruising. Sometimes, you cannot even tell if you are losing. Getting beaten in business is a slow death. Maybe your role is diminishing, or maybe you are not getting the resources you requested. Next thing you know, the excitement that made you want to work at your Company is gone. You have no idea when or if you'll get promoted, and you start getting cost of living raises. Your career and your spirit have been pummeled, but it takes place over such a long time that most do not do anything about it.

With a committed plan to improve, you can crush the untrained (I also refer to the untrained as "Naturals"). Most people in the business world are naturals. Some have better natural abilities than others. They may have great success driven by charisma, confidence, or other extraordinary traits, but I need you to know that like MMA, in the business world, every well-trained, focused person can beat every natural.

Watch Out for Group Dynamics

In the absence of clarity and resolve, it is natural to look to the group for answers. Keep in mind that the group is likely to be 70% disengaged. The disengaged are people who have rationalized that there is not an adequate return in striving to be better. When you are feeling battered and bruised, resist the tendency to look to the group for guidance. Do not get sucked into the disengaged forest. Look to your accountability group, mentors, and people walking the path to help you get back on track.

Stay Out of the Instantaneous Gratification Game

There is no straight line of dramatic improvement. You will get knocked down. Great improvements might go unrecognized. Some of your changes might be counterproductive. This is going to happen frequently. Do not give up! You are playing the long game. You are working to be dramatically better than the herd. You are striving to be a high performer in a high-performing organization. Persevere, be relentless and win!

The Value of Scarcity

In an environment where most people resist change, I want to encourage you to fall in love with improvement.

When you embrace change, success and fulfillment will embrace you back.

PRINCIPLE 5

You Get What You Tolerate

> *"What you are prepared to accept or not prepared to tolerate sets and determines the boundaries of how your life will be lived."*
> – STEVEN REDHEAD, *Life is Simply a Game*

tol·er·ate: allow the existence, occurrence, or practice of (something that one does not necessarily like or agree with) without interference.

What the Disengaged Does:

- They do not try to influence their surroundings
- They stay with bad jobs
- They compromise too often

Mediocrity Smells Bad, but You Get Used to it

Millions of people live by dairy farms, trash dumps, or sewage facilities. When visitors ask residents of these places how they get by, the standard response is, "you get used to it."

Disengagement is the stinky neighborhood of business, and 70% of all employees and almost every company, live in this stinky neighborhood. Often, I run across companies that have employees that are harmful to their operations. When I ask why the harmful employee has not been terminated, the universal reason given for retention of these horrible employees is the lack of a substitute. This is extra painful because owners know that poor performers bring down everybody, and they make it virtually impossible to build a high-performing team. I refer to this as "Eating Shit." I do not know anyone who has actually eaten shit before, but they say that you taste through your nose, so everyone knows how it would taste. When I ask the owner how the pain of keeping a bad performer equates to the concept of eating shit, most owners say it is about equal. Yet they endure without a solid plan to address the issue. They have gotten what they tolerate.

If the use of the S Word offends you to the point where you no longer think the Unicorn Principles are for you, I am sorry, but powerful imagery spurs change. I want people to associate the pain of inaction with something that they find repulsive.

Do Not Tolerate...

If you are walking the path of excellence and embracing the Unicorn Principles, you deserve to work at a company that supports your journey. Here is a recommended list of what you should not tolerate:

- A company that does not value and reward excellence
- A company that will not invest in making you better
- A company that does not care about a strong culture
- A company that does not encourage winning as a team
- A company that does not care about your personal happiness

- A company that does not have a plan for star performers to work sustainable hours.

Loyalty 2.0

It is a myth that your employer will take care of you because you have worked at the company for a long time. Staying with a company out of loyalty is a misguided notion.

Be loyal to excellence. Be loyal to a company and teammates that support your commitment to excellence. It is extremely hard to walk the path if your Company and/or your teammates are not on that path.

Save your loyalty for a great company that deserves it. If your current employer does not support your objectives, fight to help them improve. If your employer is not willing to improve, find a new employer that will. Give your loyalty to the worthy.

Purpose and Tolerance

Your purpose is more than a powerful motivator. It is critical to keeping you on track and the guidewire for forward progress. Do not let short-time wins or short-term losses gauge your success. Measure your success by how well you live your purpose. If your boss or your team gets in the way of your purpose, fix it. If you cannot fix the problem, find a new place that supports your walk on the path of excellence.

Real Job Security

Job Security is violated on a daily basis by employers with bad judgement or financial problems. I hate the idea of having to rely on an employer to "take care of me." Walking The Unicorn Path will give you real career security—the kind of job security from being so valuable that your Company will suffer significantly without you.

Always be Looking

From a traditional standpoint, the concept of an employee constantly looking for another employment opportunity is disloyal, maybe even considered reprehensible.

Employers do not want short-time employees and will not invest in their future. The purpose of constantly looking is not for you to frequently change jobs, it is to hold your employer to the highest standards.

- The better your options, the better your ability to shape your environment.
- If you do not have any career options, you have to accept what you have.
- If you wait until you are completely fed up or until you decide to quit, your career options will be limited by the need to find a replacement quickly.
- Do not feel bad – you are striving to become an incredible contributor to the success of your Company. It is your right to work for an employer that values and appreciates your excellence.

When to Jump Ship

Remember that perfection is the enemy of excellence, and change is hard. If your employer is walking The Unicorn Path, help them walk the path. Do not give up too soon. Forgive them for mistakes and deploy patience. If your employer does not care about building a high-performing team with incredible culture, great teamwork, sustainable work, and a commitment to be the best, go find a company that does.

The Value of Scarcity

By refusing to settle for mediocrity, you are striving for excellence and success. A Unicorn is distinguishably valuable. Build your skills and devote your incredible skills and effort to a company that deserves you.

PRINCIPLE 6

The Power of Love

> *"Your work is going to fill a large part of your life, and the only way to be truly satisfied is to do what you believe is great work. And the only way to do great work is to love what you do."*

– STEVE JOBS

Love /ləv/: an intense feeling of deep affection.

What the Disengaged Does:

- They love their jobs in the beginning then quickly fall out of love when their expectations are not met.
- They decide that it is not important to love what you do
- They create an environment that makes it easier for others to fall out of love.
- They suck the energy out of a company

The single biggest differentiator between the engaged and disengaged is love. Disengaged employees do not love what they do.

We win by walking The Unicorn Path (doing great work), by being passionately engaged in our jobs, by working in an organization that supports our values, and by working with a team that enhances our success. None of this can be accomplished if you do not love what you do. Ultimately, people who are not passionate about what they do will slip into the zombie walk of the 70% disengaged who view work as a way to fund their passion in other areas.

What the Unicorn Version of Work Love Looks Like

- Your work is a source of joy and happiness
- You are interested in bringing joy and happiness to others in your organization
- You look forward to going to work
- You are passionate about making your Company better
- You are passionate about making your teammates better
- Your goal is to give more than you get

The Why's – The Benefits of Loving What You Do

- It is easier to love your job – It does not cost any more to love your job. You do not have to spend any more time at work to love your job. It is developing the mindset to enjoy what you are doing. I have worked in jobs that I did not love, and it was horrible. I found myself staring at the clock and trying to will the clock to strike quitting time. It was draining, and my dissatisfaction with work diminished my happiness in my personal life. I found myself staying awake worrying about problems, issues and conflicts relating to work. I have also been involved in jobs that I love. The days would fly by. I would carry my sense of pride and happiness to my personal life. I would have more energy since I had dramatically lower stress, and I would sleep the sleep of the just.

- Jump to the front of the line – It is a great way to stand out. It is easy to spot most of the 70% of employees that are disengaged. People who love what they do stand out and go to the front of the line. Employers devote more of their resources to people who care. The objective of this book is to turn you into a high-performing Unicorn. Loving what you do is a huge part of being a Unicorn.

- It is awful to be a commodity – employees who do not love their jobs almost always fall into the disengaged categories. They get their work done, and they go home. This does not go unnoticed with employers. The less you care, the less your employer cares about you. Most of the disengaged are exiled to commodity island where you receive minimal raises (such as the 1.2% inflation raise), an uncertain career path, and a dramatic decrease in job security. Why should your employer provide you with job security if you are not passionate about what you do?

- It is easier if others help you – this is a central theme in this book, but the most sustainable way to gain success and happiness is to get help from your co-workers. The concept of duty is a myth. Whenever disengaged co-workers have a choice (which is often), they will not help you out of duty. They may help you because they must, but you can compel more people to help you by displaying passion and exuberance to what you are doing.

- Happiness is contagious – you will make your co-workers happier, and they will make you happier. Instead of a vicious cycle, you create a cycle of happiness.

The How's – How to Love Your Job

- You Have to Reach Out and Get It – you cannot wait for love to just happen or for cupid to shoot you with an arrow. You are responsible for creating the love. You need to will your way to loving your job, and more importantly, you need to will your way to overcoming the ongoing stream of obstacles. This is a great example of the difficulty of change. Logic says if loving my job jumps me ahead of 70% of the workplace, it should not be a big deal, but it will be harder than you think.

- The Power of Commitment – Apply Principle #3 – What You Commit to Gets Done. Focus on living your purpose and commit to that purpose. It sounds naïve, but the single most important thing you can do to love your job is to decide to love your job. Write it down, share it with others. Know that with commitment comes love, and with love of your job, comes happiness and prosperity.

- Accept an Imperfect Version of Love – Your love for what you do needs to be sustainable. The concept of continuous sensational gratification only applies to Hollywood and the first few weeks of a high school relationship. There will be countless times when your Company and your co-workers will not match your passion and commitment. There will be situations where your exceptional performance will go unrecognized. There will be times that you will be unjustly blamed for issues that you did not cause. Expect disappointment and work to get over it as quickly as possible. When you have a tough day, forgive yourself. You are not perfect. You might get frustrated or irritable, but as long as you choose to work at your Company, work to avoid getting sidetracked by frustration or disappointment. Strive to get back to happy. You win by being the best person, and the best people love what they do.

- Ask for Help – The high divorce rate tells us that love is wavering. Build a support team that will help you enjoy your job. Create clear and brutally honest channels to discuss issues. Get a mentor. When you have an issue, work hard to resolve the issue and get high-value feedback.

- It's A Lot Easier if Your Company and Your Boss Are on Board –To go the furthest the fastest you need help and the best help comes from the top. If your Company does not already have an employee high-performance plan with love/joy/passion as a cornerstone of excellence, lobby hard to get one. Ideally, Leadership will jump on board. A love campaign is typically a low investment, high return proposition.

- Be an Active Recruiter – Be on the constant lookout for recruits for team love/joy/passion. The fastest way to grow this team is to ask. Share your values, goals, and vision. Unfortunately, some people reject even the best offers. You are working against a system that grows disengagement. Some people have become acclimatized and will not change. Get over the disappointment of rejection and back to a position of high effectiveness. Know that your willingness to endure rejection will make you even more distinctively valuable. Your happiness, prosperity, and effectiveness will grow as your team grows.

The Where's

This may sound like heresy, but if you continue to walk the path to becoming a high-performance employee, you need to work for a company that is worthy of you. Your Company should be a valuable partner in your success.

Be loyal to organizations that strive for excellence and value your objectives and cut ties with organizations that do not. Be loyal to excellence, not tenure.

Ask these questions:

1. Does my Company have a culture that supports an environment of love/joy/passion?
2. Does my Company properly value high-performing employees?
3. Is my Company committed to winning by creating an exceptional team?
4. Is the Company committed to sustainable work hours?
5. How much do you love working at your Company?
6. Is this the right place for you to win by being the best person?

Be objective in your evaluation of your workplace. Typically, when we make decisions based on instinct or feelings, we chose the easiest path. The disengaged seeking to avoid change, make the easy choice of sticking with bad jobs. Do not give up too soon. Make sure that you put in the work to shape your Company to your needs.

More Heresy – to put yourself in the best position to move your organization in your direction, keep your options open. Continuously monitor the job market. You do not want to stay with a bad company because you do not have any other choices. The better your options, the better your success.

There is no shame in leaving a company that is not committed to your principles.

Other Considerations:

You Can Love More than One Thing – There are many who believe that love is finite and needs to be reserved for faith and family. I respect this belief but contend that love is not finite, and the more you love, the better you are at loving. I also submit that the benefits from loving your job will give you more time and resources to shower upon your loved ones in your personal life.

Loving Your Job Does Not Mean Working Crazy Hours – This book is about being the best. Having a sustainable performance system is critical to being the best. You cannot be the best if you do not have a personal life, you cannot be the best if you are not happy. Working too much curtails your performance. One day you wake up and realize it is not worth it. Work extra hours when you need to, but make sure that your standard hours give you the time to have a great life when you are not working.

Love Your Competition – Competing with co-workers is a short-term play. A large component of being a Unicorn is having others contribute to your success. Vicious co-worker competition will drive help away from you. Just by being engaged, you will be dramatically better than the disengaged. If/when (it is up to you), you become part of a company that walks The Unicorn Path, your opportunities will be plentiful. Consider that every aspect of your life will be better if you are a great employee amongst other great employees rather than an exceptional member of a poor performing team.

What to Do if People Do not Love You – It is impossible to obtain universal love. There are some people who will dislike you for being so darn happy. Often, dislike leads to conflict and dysfunctional work relationships. Do not fall into that trap. Work to optimize your effectiveness. Go out of your way to be a great teammate for people who do not like you. Do not set yourself back because of other people's problems. The best people are the best performers. Stay on track.

The Value of Scarcity

By walking The Unicorn Path, you are working to become a standout high performer. Love and happiness are incredible workplace benefits that are undervalued. Love what you do, spread the love to others, and rise above the pack.

PRINCIPLE 7

Clarity is King

"It's a lack of clarity that creates chaos and frustration. Those emotions are poison to any living goal."
– STEVE MARABOLI

clar·i·ty: the quality of being coherent and intelligible.

What the Disengaged Does:

- Sees no need for ground rules
- Guesses about what others are doing
- Makes too many assumptions
- Avoids confrontation

There is too much guessing in business, especially in the employee/employer relationship. Think about your past experiences and think about how things would change if you knew rather than had to guess. Clarity is a simple trait but not common. Knowing rather than guessing is critical to becoming a Unicorn high performer.

Where there is lack of clarity, there is uncertainty, and where there is uncertainty, there is anxiety. This is the Expectation Gap.

In the absence of clear performance standards, ambitious employees develop their own high-performance standards. Unfortunately, when an employee develops work standards without clarity, it becomes a guess:

- When an employee guesses, they are prone to misinterpreting what their employer wants.
- When employees make mistakes in interpretation, it often leads to criticism or conflict from management.
- After enough criticism or conflict, employees stop guessing.
- When employees stop guessing, they stop trying to improve.
- When employees stop trying to improve, they become disengaged

Some employees are better than others at guessing, but no one guesses perfectly. This principle is about using Clarity to stand out and excel.

Fine Dining

Imagine going to a nice restaurant to celebrate an anniversary. You sit down, you order, the entrée comes, and something is not quite right with your food. Different people have different reactions. Some people get angry and make their anger known to the waiter. Some people calmly ask for their food to be fixed, and some people pick at their food and resolve to make it the last time they dine at the restaurant. The anxiety increases since the patron has no idea how the waiter will react. Will the waiter get angry too? Will the manager comp your meal? Will the kitchen abuse your re-worked order? Even at the best restaurants, there are far too many instances of dissatisfied customers. Here's where clarity could come to the rescue.

Reset the same scene, except when your waiter greets you, he or she says, "Thank you for visiting Chez Unicorn. Our goal is to make every experience fantastic. If anything does not meet your standards, please bring the issue to my attention as quickly as possible. We will happily take care of the problem. We want you to leave here with great memories, and we want to be the first place you think of when you want to have a special night. Do you have any questions regarding our service policy?"

In this instance, the waiter's initial greeting would:

- Provide ground rules for customer complaints – by agreeing to the rules, the customer will be less likely to blow their top with an issue since they have been invited to bring a problem to the waiter's attention.

- By opening the lines of communication, customer service issues flow faster. This gives the restaurant more time to fix the problem. The next best thing to not having a problem is fixing the problem quickly.

- Customer service clarity aligns with the restaurant's purpose of being a place that customers love and come back.

No matter what you do, you will never be perfect. In the absence of ground rules, you have no idea how people will respond to any mistakes you make. You can use ground rules to gain critical information that will allow you to clean up an issue with minimal anxiety. Since repeat business is critical for fine dining restaurants, this kind of clarity is a distinctive advantage over the competition.

Here are examples of how clarity can help you become a high-performing employee:

<u>Role Clarity</u> – Know your job requirements – many companies have written job descriptions. This is a good start but not enough. As we will discuss in communication, written words do not always convey context. Memorize your written job description but keep asking questions and learning until your role is clear to you. Continue to amend your written job description to gain even more role clarity.

<u>Inquiry Clarity</u> – When I started my career with an international CPA firm, the rule was do not ask for help or clarification until you have done everything to figure it out yourself. While it was not a fantastic way for me to learn my role, I valued the clarity. Knowledge is power and clarity is knowledge. Work with your employer and your team to set rules for asking questions.

<u>Performance Clarity</u> – Work with management and your team to determine the standards of high performance. Doing your best is good. Knowing what your employer thinks is exceptional is far better. Work to refine your standards to improve clarity. To be great, you need to know what great is. The most extreme example of lack of Performance Clarity is when an employee gets fired and expresses anger and frustration. When an employee knows exactly where he or she stands, they get out of the toughest guessing game of all. Whenever possible, strive to get a high frequency review process. Getting deep feedback once or twice a year is not good enough. I recommend that you get a 5-minute review weekly, a 1-hour review monthly, and a 2-3 hour review quarterly. Receiving frequent standardized feedback is a fantastic way to get better.

<u>Core Values Clarity</u> – In great organizations, Core Values are the Bill of Rights for excellence. Unfortunately, most organizations do not have frequent ongoing discussions on key aspects of these values. Also, many companies have one-word core values such as integrity or excellence. There is a serious lack of clarity in a one-word core

value. Have discussions with management and your team until you have a strong grasp of the true intents of your Company's core values.

Mission and Vision Clarity – Most employees do not know their company's mission and vision. This occurs largely because most companies do not talk enough about their mission and vision. In order to optimize Principle #2 – The Power of Purpose, you need to have a clear idea of your Company's purpose (mission and vision) and be able to align your efforts with the mission. Do not wait for people to teach you. Be proactive. Take the responsibility for your clarity. Memorize the written mission statement and vision and seek out meaningful conversations to learn the true intent and purpose of your Company's mission statement and vision.

Receiving Feedback Clarity – There is no better way to improve than to receive feedback, especially feedback that stings. Work with your employer and your team to set the ground rules for delivering you tough feedback. Whenever possible, set up a feedback system that avoids heated words. Like a restaurant, there are too many instances where people suppress their feedback. When people suppress their feedback, they are moving further away from contributing to your success.

Giving Feedback Clarity – You can have a great team or you can try to outwork the problem. As we have previously discussed, the long hours required to outwork your problems is not sustainable. Continuous long hours leads to diminished happiness, which leads to a waning pursuit of excellence. To win as a team, you have to improve as a team. Providing timely, tough feedback is a critical component of improvement. In the absence of ground rules, feedback is typically greeted angrily. After a couple of "mind your blankety blank business" comments, most employees stop providing tough feedback. They receive a lousy payoff for their trouble. While delivering tough feedback is never easy, it works when both parties have agreed to an effective way of providing this information. We will discuss more about this in Principle #9 Conflict is the Competitive Edge.

Interruption Clarity – Interruptions are a formidable enemy to committed focus and work momentum. You need to establish Interruption Clarity to optimize your work output and to minimize your impact from interrupting others. Set up ground rules that block out time for intense, productive work. Encourage others to do the same. Set rules for exceptions and make it clear when you are immediately available for interruption.

Career Clarity – Many employees have no idea when they will receive their next raise. Most employees do not know how much they will receive in their next raise. Most employees do not have a clear idea of what they need to do to make more. Hoping for the best is not a strategy. Work with your employer to build a map of where you are going, what you need to do to get there, and what you will get paid along the way. Blend patience and persistence in this process as your Company might not know all of the answers immediately. Encourage your employer to set up a plan that shows your career path, the timing, the milestones needed to hit, and the expected compensation as you progress along the way.

Do Not Assume

It hurts to be described as prejudice but in fact, everyone pre-judges. The tendency to assume is hardcoded into us. Speculating was a valuable protection mechanism when turning the wrong corner could get our caveman ancestors eaten. When we assume we are making decisions without all the facts. Whenever possible, especially when it is important, avoid the assumption shortcuts and gather the necessary facts to make a knowledgeable decision.

The Value of Clarity

Striving for clarity is common sense that is infrequently applied. Clarity is a trait that will cause you to absolutely stand out from the pack. In your pursuit of clarity, do not be deterred by tradition or group thinking. Ask the questions, carve the trails, and be strong when you get resistance.

PRINCIPLE 8

You Can Have Systems or Chaos

| *"In the absence of a system, you defer to someone else's system."*
– BART DUNNE

sys·tem: A set of things working together as parts of a mechanism or an interconnecting network. A set of principles or procedures according to which something is done, an organized scheme or method.

What the Disengaged Does:

- They apply their standards to their actions.
- They do not adapt to the systems of others/core values
- They wing it

Systems are the delivery mechanism for clarity, improvement, teamwork, and performance. The alternative to systems in the workplace is common sense which is neither common nor a system. In an environment of uncertainty, people will guess the correct solution, and typically, their guess is not aligned with the most

119

effective objective. It is rare that a company will talk about building high performers and even rarer that a company will have a system to develop high performers. In an environment that lacks clarity, the ambitious have to guess as to what it takes to be a high performer. Business books talk about getting everyone to row the boat in the same direction, but in the absence of an effective performance system, each person will decide how fast to row and what direction to row in. Employees often look to the group to help when they are not certain, but keep in mind that in most companies, the majority of most groups are disengaged. Everybody rowing in different directions and different speeds might strike you as an unacceptable level of chaos, but these conditions exist in most businesses every minute of every day.

Deploy systems for critical components of your job and your career path.

It Is not a System if Others Cannot Understand it

If people cannot understand a system, they cannot follow it. The easier to understand, the more likely people are to follow.

Even if it is just for you, a system needs to be clear and understandable. Remember you cannot receive help if people cannot figure out how to help you.

Your Systems Need to Align With Key Objectives

To get the most out of your systems, make sure that you are headed in the right direction. Invoke Principle #2 – The Power of Purpose and get extra systems power from your purpose. Make your systems meaningful by making sure your systems line up with your Company's mission and/or your professional purpose. Use your systems to crush your goals by optimizing effectiveness, focus, and cooperation to get the most important stuff done.

Documentation is Essential and Not Enough

Documenting your systems is crucial to providing an understandable and repeatable process. Many companies think that they are done once their systems are documented, but it is only the start. Documentation is not enough. Think about driving on the freeway. There is a thick book of traffic laws. Every driver must pass a test. There are traffic signs posted prominently, yet there are multiple ways to drive. The next time someone cuts you off or follows you too closely, chalk it up to their adoption of a different driving system.

Systems Need to Live in our Hearts and Minds

It is extremely rare when written documentation conveys the kind of emotion that compels passionate loyalty and commitment. To build a highly effective system, you need to capture the hearts and minds of everyone involved with the system.

- Live the system – With documentation as the foundation, you need a recurring and incessant tempo. You need to constantly discuss your system and point out instances of success and failure in system execution. Encourage others to give you feedback on your systems every chance you have. If people are not teasing you for incessantly talking about your systems, you are not talking about them enough.
- Publicize your systems – Systems are critical to sustainable team-oriented success. Treat them as such. Be a raving fan.

Tell the world the benefits of your system. Shout from the rooftop.

- Celebrate – Go out of your way to point out the successes that come from your systems. Share stories of how systems are enhancing your success and moving you down the path of excellence and high performance.

Systems Are Change

Any new system is change, and with change, you will get resistance. People who are used to working alone will resist the team aspect. The disengaged will resist any change to their routine. Most of the resistance will be passive. People will smile, nod their heads, say yes, but they will resist.

- Be Persistent - You will encounter countless hurdles, do not quit. You are walking the path of excellence. It is not always easy.
- Be Patient – Change takes time. Stay on the path. Anger and frustration will not help.
- Get Help – Look for champions in senior management. Recruit the passionately engaged to be on your team.

Systems Need to Be Dynamic

Your system is not a casserole. You cannot set it and forget it. Like every aspect of life, systems are not perfect. There will be instances when you will get minimal gratification on the operation of your systems. You will experience outright failure. If you want to walk the path of excellence and be a high performer, you need dynamic systems.

- Always look to improve your system. Keep evaluating new possibilities. I am not a golfer, but golf provides a great example. A golf swing is a system. Success in a golf swing comes from being consistently repeatable. Most professional golfers have been swinging a club since they were kids. In spite of their success and experience, the best golfers continuously work to improve their swing system.
- Constantly assess the effectiveness or your system. Build an accountability system where objective results are measured to determine the success. TRACK→ ASSESS → ADJUST
- Ask for help from both inside your group and outside your group. Build your system from the best ideas.

Systems Go Far Beyond Tasks

Everything is a system. Here are some examples of how systems can enhance your performance:

- Conflict – We have already started talking about this in Unicorn Principle #7 – Clarity is King, and in Unicorn Principle #9 Conflict is the Ultimate Advantage, we will go into this in detail, but it bears emphasis. It takes a system to master the power of conflict.
- Raises and Promotion – The uncertainty of compensation and advancement is a big reason why employee disengagement is rampant. How can you stay engaged if you must guess critical aspects of your career? Too often, ambition perishes when guesses turn to disappointment. There are no rules that prevent you from building a system to understand when you will receive raises and promotions and what you need to do to receive them.

- Firing – If you are reading this book, you are a leader or a future leader. As a leader, you will be required to terminate others. It is a painfully difficult and disruptive process. In the absence of a firing system, you have a whole lot of guessing in the firing process. In this environment, the terminated party is typically surprised and angry, and the manager is reluctant to engage in such a painful process. Build a system of clarity so that everyone, especially poor performers, know exactly where they stand.

The Value of Scarcity

Operational excellence is an incredible trait. Systems development is critical to operational excellence. You are striving to be a uniquely valuable member of the workforce. Make mastery of systems part of your skill set.

PRINCIPLE 9

Conflict is the Ultimate Competitive Advantage

"For good ideas and true innovation, you need human interaction, conflict, argument and debate."
– MARGARET HEFFERNAN

con·flict: be incompatible or at variance; clash.

What the Disengaged Does:

- They avoid conflict
- They get angry and yell
- They complain to others rather than confront the problem

The core of high performance is improvement, and the best way to improve is to receive deep, insightful, and frequent feedback. Even if it hurts. Live a life where the truth is good enough. Conflict should not be a workplace enemy. Make mediocrity and indifference the enemy.

Difficult Things Must be Said

There are three ways to have difficult conversations:

1. Avoiding Arguments– It is human nature to avoid pain and optimize pleasure. Difficult discussions are typically considered painful. It gets worse for the brave who wade into difficult conversations unprepared and receive an angry response from their feedback. When the well-intentioned are met with anger, they tend to shy away from getting involved.

2. Heated Arguments – People who get angry and release their anger on others are not effective. When you get mad, you are trading effectiveness for a very short-term emotional payoff. It is extremely rare when angry screaming makes a situation better.

3. Engage in Great and Productive Conversations – Imagine the helpful advice you will receive if you learn to welcome difficult feedback. Visualize how much you can help others if you learn to deliver tough feedback in an effective manner.

Some of my biggest regrets come from what I did not say.

Steps for Productive Conflict

1. Resolve to be Great at Conflict – Invoke the power of Principle #2 – The Power of Purpose. Use the power to resolve to be excellent at conflict. Becoming great at conflict is a huge change for most. Invoke the power of purpose to get through the pain of change.

2. Create a System – A documented, well-crafted system will bring clarity and accountability to the issue.

3. Start with You – Invite tough feedback before you start delivering it to others. Go out of your way to react positively. Thank people for helping you be great.

4. Get Help – Everything is easier with help. Present your conflict plan to leadership. Work to get champions on your team. Convert one at a time. Do not hesitate to whip out your copy of the Unicorn Principles to get others to understand what you are trying to do.

5. Tempo – The more often you have difficult conversations, the better you will get at delivering the hard truth.

6. Persist – The implementation of a conflict management system will be packed full of challenges. Despite the best system and the best implementation, people will get their feelings hurt, and angry arguments will emerge. Some people will mock you, and some will avoid involvement, do not give up. You are on the right path.

7. Publicize the Process – The Unicorn Path has a template documenting how you wish to give and receive difficult feedback. You can request this document by emailing info@UnicornPath.com. Complete the document and put it in a prominent spot in your work area.

8. Celebrate – When you get great results from conflict, have a celebration. Make public declarations thanking people for giving you tough feedback. Tell stories to anyone who will listen detailing how receiving tough feedback has made you better.

9. Be Vulnerable – Do not be afraid to talk about setbacks in this process. Vulnerability is powerful. People want to help the vulnerable. Sharing your mistakes will make people want to help you get better.

10. Decide What to Tolerate – Despite your best efforts, some people will not join in on the plan. Expect strong resistance.

If it gets to the point that your Company's culture rejects difficult conversations, work to change the culture. If you cannot see victory on the horizon, look for another company to deploy your excellence.

The Elements of a Conflict System

- Focus on Being Effective - Fight to avoid an angry response. If necessary, take a second to calm down. Anger triggers a rebellious response. If you get angry, you lose the argument before it starts.

- Tonality matters – Tonality is more important than words in communication. For optimal effectiveness, use a relaxed, nurturing tone.

- Be Courageous – By deploying a conflict system, you are blasting out of your comfort zone. It gets scary out there. Be brave and go forward knowing that if you wimp out, you are stifling improvement for you, your team, and your Company.

- Ask Permission – Whenever possible, ask the receiver for permission to have a tough conversation. It may sound like a trivial formality, but asking for permission greatly improves the way the message will be received. When the receiver gives you permission to have a conflict discussion, it makes them a better listener and less likely to get angry with what they hear. If they say no when you ask permission, move on. Do not engage in conflict with those who don't care about receiving tough comments.

- State Your Purpose and Make it About Them – The purpose of every difficult conversation should be to make the receiver better and to make the company better. State this purpose and state it in a calm and supportive manner.

- Avoid Criticizing – You do not accomplish anything by making someone feel bad. Do not make it personal.

- Discuss Next Steps – Talk about what needs to be done going forward to get better. Set an action plan with goals and accountability to implement improvements.

- Clear the Air – The goal is for none of the parties to leave the discussion angry. At the end of the discussion, ask if the goal has been met. If the goal has not been met, work with urgency to get back on track.

Whenever Possible Set Up Ground Rules in Advance

Sun Tzu in, "The Art of War," stated that "Every battle is won or lost before it is ever fought." Make no mistake, implementing a decision of productive conflict will be a battle. A key to winning this battle is setting up your ground rules in advance. Meet with people you work with and get them to agree to the ground rules before you enter a potentially volatile conversation.

Passive-Aggressive Behavior is a Culture Killer

I used to guess the definition of the term passive-aggressive. Here is a definition I found on the internet so that others do not have to guess.

Passive-aggressive behaviors are those that involve acting indirectly aggressive rather than directly aggressive. Passive-aggressive people regularly exhibit resistance to requests or demands from family and other individuals often by procrastinating, expressing sullenness, or acting stubborn.

Most businesses treasure harmony at the expense of the productive discussion. Companies rarely encourage productive, difficult conversations and even fewer train people how to have such conversations. As a result, companies are facilitators of passive-aggressive behavior.

From my experience, passive-aggressive behavior has another attribute – Venting/Talking Behind Someone's Back. Talking behind a person's back has no positive value and can destroy teamwork and culture. Remember, the biggest problems you will have will come from things you did not say. Make a habit of never saying anything about someone you would not say directly to them and encourage others to do the same.

More on Effective Conflict

- Pick Your Battles - Only Use Conflict for a Purpose – You do not have unlimited conflict bullets. Do not waste them on things that do not support your objectives of being a high performer and winning as a team. Do not get to the point that people are ducking you because you are the "argumentative one."

- Adjust to Your Audience – When you need to have difficult conversations, adjust the level of the conversation to your audience. When you are having a challenging discussion with someone for the first few times, work extra hard to deliver your messages softly.

- Not Everyone Wants to Play – Conflict resolution is an amazing tool. So amazing that it will be easy to want everyone to have the gift of effective conflict. Remember that not everyone wants to be converted. When you get hesitation, push back, or passive avoidance, let up on the conflict throttle. Do not get frustrated. Understand that this is a big change and not everybody wants to change.

- Being Effective is More Important Than Being Right – Even when you are absolutely right, being right isn't the most important thing. You are a future Unicorn. You do not need to win every argument. You do not need to correct every error. Your path is to get better, make others better, and have others make you better. The need to always prove that you are right often conflicts with this goal.

- Everybody Needs to Feel Better When it is Over – When you start a tough conflict-oriented conversation, make it a goal for everyone to leave the conversation feeling better than when the conversation started. Consider stating that the goal for everyone is leaving the conversation feeling better than when you began the conversation. Delivering the valuable truth is essential but delivering it in a manner that enriches all is a gift.

The Value of Scarcity

The highest and best form of success comes when you receive the help of others. A team can accomplish so much more than an individual. Improvement is critical to great a great team. Tough feedback is critical to improvement. Master the skills to engage in tough conversations and gain an incredibly valuable and distinctive skill.

PRINCIPLE 10

Change Your World with Communication

| *"The art of communication is the language of leadership."*
– JAMES HUMES

com·mu·ni·ca·tion: the imparting or exchanging of information or news

What the Disengaged Does:

- They bury their nose in their phone
- They do not value communication
- They are not working to get better at meaningful conversations.

It took me too long to realize that **success in all aspects of our life comes from the quality of our conversations.** The value of great communication goes way beyond work. The single most important factor in my relationships with my loved ones and friends is communication.

Most employees, whether entry-level laborers or MBA's, are not familiar with the nuances of communication. Most people do not work on their communication skills. They go with what they developed naturally. Strong communication skills are extremely valuable and will make you stand out from the disengaged.

The tools in this chapter will set you apart. Tools that you will be working to develop that others are not.

It Starts with Body Language

Body language is more important than words. In a book published in 1970 by Ray L. Birdwhistell, he suggested that 55% of communication is physiology. Physiology pertains to our gestures, mannerisms, and movements. The best way to improve your communication is to improve your body language.

The first step is to become aware of your natural body language. Where do you place your hands, what is your posture, how do you sit, how do you place your legs?

Next, pay attention to how others move. Ask for feedback from people you care about. Watch others and adopt their best mannerisms. Start incorporating the best practices of others into your own body language.

Rather than guessing what body language means, consider mirroring the body language of others. We live in a tribal society, and people like others who are like them. When they move forward, you move forward; when they cross their legs, you cross your legs. Body language works at the subconscious level. Do not worry about someone recognizing your mirroring, especially after a little practice.

Pay attention to the cues you provide to others through facial expressions and bodily movement.

Keys to improve Body Language:

- Do not worry about failing or changing. It will diminish your progress. Jump in and get after it.
- Practice, and keep practicing. It will not happen fast
- Red Team this – get your Red Team to give you feedback every time they see you.
- You are never done learning. Always study the body language of both yourself and others. Read books about body language.
- Get Help – ask others for feedback and coaching.
- Do a Pregame – when you are going into an important meeting, spend a couple of seconds to determine what components of body language you want to focus on.
- Visualize how your life will change if you can dramatically improve the most important aspect of communication.

Tonality is More Important than Words

In his previously referenced book, Ray L. Birdwhistell said that 38% of communication is the tonality of our voice when we speak.

Mirroring also applies tonality. People like people who sound like themselves. If they speak faster than you, pick up the pace, if they speak slow, you slow down. Listen for some of their favorite words and use them in the conversation.

Confidence is great, but if your tonality is perceived as arrogant, you are not likely to have a great conversation. This will be discussed further when we address vulnerability but adding a little humility to your tonality is a great way to stay out of the arrogant territory.

A critical component in providing highly effective tonality is to avoid natural triggers. Our tonality triggers behavior in others. When we speak in a critical tone it triggers anger. When we are nurturing, it triggers relaxed, open responses. In the absence of a committed effort to change, most of us respond to the same triggers. When you are triggered into an angry tone, the conversation gets worse. When you speak in an angry tone, you are responding to your natural programming and ignoring your objective of having an outstanding conversation. You can defy your natural behavior with commitment and resolve; it is the essence of improvement.

Keys to Improving Your Tonality:

- Like most things, the first step is recognizing your need to improve.
- Determine your desired outcome – Strive to always deploy a nurturing or authentic intellectual tonality. Throw out all the critical tonalities that hinder communication.
- It takes practice driven by commitment and resolve to power through failure and uncomfortable experiences.
- Watch the results and adjust – see what works and what does not work and adjust.
- Invite people to provide you with tough feedback directed at your tonality.
- Believe that great conversations are the most critical component of success and resolve to be the best.

E-Mail, Texts and Letters

If physiology is 55% of communication and tonality is 38% of communication, that only leaves 7% for words. Feel free to debate the breakdown, but I hope you acknowledge the importance of using physiology and tonality in communication.

When you e-mail or write a report, you lose all benefits of physiology and tonality. Do not use e-mail for important communication, especially if the words can be construed as critical.

Here is the hierarchy:

- Communication that is critical – communicate in person and get the full benefit of your physiology and tonality skills.
- Moderately important communication – if you cannot be there in person, use the phone and at least get the benefit of tonality.
- Basic Communication – e-mail is great for emotionless interactions such as setting appointments.

When you send an e-mail for a critical subject, you are deciding that avoiding conflict is more important than effectively conveying your thoughts. I have seen too many instances where a misconstrued e-mail turns into a huge issue.

Keys to Improving Your Written Communication:

- Set up ground rules that you will never send out an angry e-mail. Here's an example: "Please do not interpret any anger or frustration in any of my e-mails. If I have a difficult issue, I will do it face to face or over the phone in the worst case."
- Do not wimp out when you have a problem. This book is loaded with tools to help you effectively manage conflict.
- Limit written communication to transactional language

- Assume that someone will misconstrue a controversial aspect of your writing.
- When in doubt, ask for advice on sending the communication.

Make it About Them when You Talk

A big part of communication is getting people to listen to and absorb your thoughts and ideas. The subconscious part of your brain (the elephant) has incredible control over your operating systems. Your subconscious mind naturally filters what you hear and disregards most aspects of conversations that are not specifically intended for you. This is the primary reason why studies have reported that only about 20% of the average conversation is retained.

To gain the incredible advantage of receiving increased retention of what others hear, go out of your way to make the conversation about them. This is easier said than done since the same subconscious drives you to speak about you.

Keys to improve Making it About Them:

- Assess your status. When you leave a conversation, think about how often you spoke about yourself and how often you spoke about the other person.
- Red Team this – get your Red Team to give you feedback on this issue every time you meet.
- Do a Pregame – when you are going into an important meeting, spend a couple of seconds to make a conscious decision to make the conversation about them.
- Keep the 20% retention number in mind and visualize how your life will improve as your retention number increases.

Make it About Them when You Listen

You have a subconscious too! In the absence of doing something about it, you will only retain approximately 20% of what others say. When you are in a conversation, make it about them. Rip down your filters and make what they have to say more important than what you have to say.

Keys to improve Your Listening:

- Consciously strive to hear everything said.
- Do a Pregame –spend a couple of seconds to focus on stripping away your listening filter.
- Decide that the other parties in your conversations are more important than you.
- Think about the benefits of being a premier listener.

We Filter What We Say

Filtering of information also applies to what we say. Often, we do not say what we want to say because we do not think we are going to get the results we want. A lot of people think withholding our thoughts is good manners. It is indisputable that saying things to destroy the feelings of others is horribly counterproductive. Alternatively, withholding thoughts is a detriment to people you care about. Filtering what you say chips away at your authenticity and your integrity.

Here is the key to ripping down this filter – *You Can Say Anything to Anybody if You Ask Permission and Ask the Right Way.* I typically start tough conversations with, "do I have permission to talk about a very sensitive subject?" When I get the yes, I use softening tonality to suggest that "I'm giving you this feedback because I want to make you better."

Keys to strip away filters in your speech:

- Wade in slowly, practice on low-risk relationships like counter people at stores.
- Forgive yourself when lowering your filter does not work. Your objective is not perfect responses, it is a dramatic improvement of your communication skills.
- Check your ego at the door. The biggest problems occur when there is even the slightest hint of you trying to be better than they are.
- You can clean up almost everything.
- Run ideas for delivering tough comments by a mentor.
- Imagine how much better your conversations will be if you can deal in the absolute truth.

Filter Wrap Up

Imagine the advantage you will have if more of the words you say are retained. Imagine the advantage of being a better listener. Finally, imagine if you are able to deliver more of your thoughts. A big part of quality communication is having conversations that sound like we are talking to friends. A big part of the friend conversation process is stripping away the filters.

Emotion Compels Action

This section focuses on how to invoke emotion in a conversation.

I was conditioned to speak succinctly in intellectual terms. This is referred to as transactional language such, A+B=C—I want to go to the store. When I speak in transactional language, the listener hears the word in their conscious mind (The Ant).

To get emotion, to speak to the elephant, you need to give emotion and convey it in all aspects of communication. Use more why's and fewer hows and whats.

Keys to improve Triggering Emotion via Communication:

- Assess your current status – are you an emotional person or are you more logical?
- Decide you want to improve.
- Start paying attention to emotion in communications when you speak with others. Incorporate the best aspects into your communication tools.
- Do not fear embarrassment or discomfort, fear being ordinary.
- Pregame is huge – this is the affirmation that drives the change. Spend a moment to think about how you are going to focus on emotion.

Compliments Matter

Mark Twain once said, "I can live for two months on a good compliment." According to a study by Nagoya Institute of Technology (thank goodness for the internet) compliments activate a region of the brain known as the striatum that encourages people to perform better.

For most of my life, I was frugal with compliments. I was so competitive that I felt that complimenting someone was putting them ahead of me. After lots of training and practice, I finally came to realize that the better I made someone else feel, the better my life was.

Never, never, never give someone a false compliment. It is a huge setback, and you lose integrity and authenticity.

I practiced until my complimenting got better. I started seeing the beauty in everything. Even though I practiced my skills, my goal was not to develop a catalog of standardized compliments to use as necessary. My objective was to give specific, meaningful compliments delivered naturally at the right time.

My emphasis on complimenting had another remarkable impact on my life. I learned to genuinely appreciate others. It is much easier for people to appreciate me if I appreciate them.

To get started, pay attention to conversations when others are speaking and watch the reaction when a great compliment is delivered.

Practice everywhere. Practice when you order food, practice on your dog, practice in the mall, just keep practicing. Do not give up, there is always discomfort with this type of change. It will not feel natural – Do not Stop! You will give a bad compliment – Do not Stop! You will get tired of practicing – Do not Stop! It is a small price to pay for how much better you will make others feel and how much more they will like you.

Story Telling

As you passionately walk The Unicorn Path, you will start learning from great communicators. If you want your words to stick, if you want your words to live in the hearts and minds of others for years to come, tell an exceptional story.

Stories do not have to take long. You can tell a remarkable story in 30 seconds.

Here are the key elements:

- Speak in emotional terms (use why's)
- Avoid transactional language such as 2+2 = 4.
- Pick out key details and give them life – Chekhov said, "Don't tell me that the moon is shining; show me the glint of light on broken glass."
- Use your tonality and body language tools.
- Keep your ego down – you do not need to be a star.
- Humor is a great component of a great story; vulnerability is even better.
- Do not disqualify yourself before you get started – If you are not a good natural storyteller, do not pass because it makes you uncomfortable. Work to be the best.
- Find master storytellers (both in person and online), watch others, and fall in love with learning about great stories.
- Forgive yourself when you tell a bad story. Forgive yourself for telling 10 bad stories.
- Practice, practice with friends, practice with strangers, just practice.
- Focus on the value of having your words stick. Think about how valuable and distinctive your communication will be if your conversations will be remembered for years.

Use Committed Language

Speak with conviction. Avoid using non-committed words such as try, hope, and maybe. Using these words will diminish your powers of communication and weaken your ability to commit.

The More People Talk the More They Tend to Like You

Consider deploying the 30/70 rule. The goal for great conversation is that you should talk 30% of the time and let the other person talk 70%. The guiding principle is that the less you talk, the more people will like you.

The key to getting people to talk more is to ask questions rather than make statements. When you make statements, you typically are talking about yourself. Statements also make you vulnerable to assumptions.

Unless there is a time constraint, avoid interrupting someone when they are talking. A great technique to reduce interruptions is deploying a 1 count. When someone pauses, count to one before responding.

The Value of Scarcity

Let every time you see someone with their nose buried in their phone inspire you to become an amazing communicator. Communication is a key attribute of leaders and team builders. The best communicators will have the best success.

PRINCIPLE 11

Win as a Team

| *"Alone we can do so little, together we can do so much."*
– HELEN KELLER

Team: A group of individuals working together to achieve their goal.

What the Disengaged Does:

- They Undervalue Teamwork
- They Have No Focus on Improving Others Around Them
- They Keep to Themselves

It is very seductive to be a Superman (or Superwoman). Think about the characteristics of Superman – invincibility, incredible strength, x-ray vision, flight. It is easy for the ambitious to want to "superman" his or her way through their career. It feels great to have business superpowers, to stand out and feel indispensable, to be the hero on the job.

People who "superman" in business are extraordinary performers:

- They work long hours
- They passionately focus on tasks
- They are highly motivated

Here are the problems with Superman mode:

- By going it alone supermen, you are implicitly rejecting others. This pushes the other members of your Company further away.
- Supermanning is not sustainable. Supermen burn out.
- It is difficult to advance if no one knows how to do what you do.
- It is hard to be happy if you are outworking your problems. A big component of a Unicorn's success comes from being happy.

How Do You Eat an Elephant?

This question is often used to describe how to approach accomplishing a big project, but the standard answer of "one bite at a time" is wrong. Elephants weigh approximately 15,000 pounds and yield approximately 5,000 pounds of meat. If you ate a pound of elephant meat a day, it would take you over 13 years to eat the whole elephant. By that time, you would likely go crazy, and the meat would spoil. The real answer to the question "how do you eat an elephant" is to get help.

Make the Change

It takes a leap of faith to commit to have your success coming from the help of others rather than by your own direct efforts, but the results are worth it. You will be trading the value of being indispensable with the value of being a master at team dynamics. In the long run, the payoff is far better going with the team.

Nature vs. Nurture

Some people are naturally better at working in team environments than others. With the right reasons and commitment, anyone can become great at team building. No one is naturally a master of teamwork; some people just have a head start.

Characteristics of Outstanding Teams and Teammates

Commitment – The more you rely on others, the more you risk problems. When a teammate makes a mistake or misses a deadline, it is a natural response to superman the problem. Relying on others subjects you to frustration, embarrassment, and criticism. When things are going bad due to the performance of others, do not surrender your commitment to teamwork. Walk the challenging path of becoming a master team builder knowing your life and career will be fantastic once you get through the pain. Take the pain to train. Do not wimp out!

Clarity – a huge cause of failure is when people do not clearly understand their tasks and roles. Take the time to make sure that each team member has a great understanding of their daily role.

Project Plan – Do not wait to unwrap the gift to see what you got. If you get to a deadline and get surprised by your teammates' results, it is your fault. Create a timeline with checkpoints to verify that everything is on target and on time.

Be Someone People Want to Help – Do not rely on duty for others to help you. Even in great environments, teammates have incredible discretion as to how they will help you. Be nice, treat everyone from the CEO to the mail clerk as a friend. While Unicorns have high standards, get good at forgiving. There is no value in making people feel awful.

Give More than You Get – There are givers, and there are takers. Do not be a taker, and do not get into quid pro quo. Go out of your way to give more than you get. Constantly be on the lookout for ways to help others. Keep helping even if some co-workers never reciprocate. Not only are you being a nice person, but you are also invoking the Law of Reciprocity. The Law of Reciprocity states that when someone does something nice for you, you will have a deep-rooted psychological urge to do something nice in return. Kindness is a great investment. Studies have shown that the Law of Reciprocity triggers incredible gains for the initial giver.

Practice Passionate Personal Accountability – The truth is critical, but before you assign blame to others, look at every aspect of your own performance and go out of your way to take the blame. If someone on your team failed, think about what you could have done to avoid the problem. Blaming others can kill a culture of performance. Unicorns deploy high personal accountability, which leads to an environment where issues can be comfortably addressed.

Be Vulnerable – Vulnerability is an exceptional under-utilized superpower. Most people, especially men, want to portray uber confidence and invulnerability. Confidence is important, but do not hesitate to point out your short-comings. Ask for help. Confess to not knowing it all. Own your mistakes. Apologize more. Most people go out of their way help the vulnerable, and most people assume that the invincible do not need help. Increasing your vulnerability is a major change to the operating system of many. This change will be hard. Knuckle down, work through the awkward transition, and your new vulnerability will help you blossom soon enough.

Trust – Without trust, you cannot have a great team. The single biggest thing you can do to become trusted is to give trust. Do not wait for someone to do something extraordinary to start trusting them. Start by trusting people. Do not be quick to dismiss trust. If someone is not meeting your expectations, work to get that person back on track. Commitment, personal accountability, and vulnerability are critical components of trust. Communication is important as well. Have conversations about trust and ask what you can do to gain trust in others. Confidence conveys competence which leads to trust but blend your confidence with authenticity and vulnerability to build the highest level of trust.

Make Others Better – Making others better is a core Unicorn trait. As a Unicorn, your value as a high performer will come from being dramatically better at the most important aspects of business. Start by developing a passion for helping others on your team.

Preach the Value of the Team – Teams are the foundation of your success. Talk about how the team is contributing to your life— express gratitude for your team. Go out of your way to celebrate success. The more that teammates like the team, the better they will perform.

Tough Feedback is the Cornerstone of Improvement – The best way to help someone is to give them of tough feedback as referred to in Principle #9 Conflict Is the Ultimate Competitive Advantage. In addition to courageously delivering the tough truth, invite others to deliver tough feedback to you.

Get Help – When you come across people who display great team skills, ask them for advice. Read books and watch videos. The nuances of team dynamics are infinitesimal.

Dealing with Bad Teammates

It is likely that you will experience teammates who do not hold up their end. Here are some suggestions for dealing with them:

- Do not get upset or disappointed. With 70% employee disengagement, you are more likely than not to have some poor performers on your team
- Do not yell at them, it does not help
- Tell them the hard truth in an effective manner
- Do not let frustration hold back your performance
- Take the problems as an opportunity to shine by picking up the slack
- Revise the plan and distribute updated timelines and duties to other teammates
- Feed the facts of the poor performance into your Company's accountability system

Dealing with a Bad Culture

Invoke Principle #5 – You Get What You Tolerate. If your Company's leadership is not interested in employee development and building great teams, you may not be in the right place. Do not give up easily. There are no perfect environments. Work to change the culture. Be the shining light of inspiration with your daily high-performance. If you ultimately conclude that your Company is not interested in developing people and great teams, find a new job. You are on The Unicorn Path. It will not be hard to find a new job.

The Value of Scarcity

As you meet people in the business world, ask them what they are doing to improve their teamwork skills. In most cases, the answer will be nothing. Occasionally, someone will talk about reading a book, but most are not focused on getting better. Most people are deploying the same skills that they have used for years. Unicorns are distinctive high performers. Unicorns are constantly working to improve key aspects of their skills. Being an exceptional teammate is one of the most valuable skills of a Unicorn. While your competition is relying on their natural skills, you're learning the mastery of teamwork, which will vault you into the top performer level.

PRINCIPLE 12

The Less You Fear, the Better Your Life

"Don't fear failure so much that you refuse to try new things. The saddest summary of a life contains three descriptions: could have, might have, and should have."
– LOUIS E. BOONE

Fear /ˈfir/: an unpleasant emotion caused by the belief that someone or something is dangerous, likely to cause pain, or a threat.

What the Disengaged Does:

- They Fear rejection
- They Shrink from challenges
- They do not see any benefit in taking chances

There is nothing unnatural about being fearful. Fear is instinctually hard-coded into us. Fear lives in the subconscious mind, which makes it extremely powerful. There is no waking up one day and deciding not to fear anything. To enhance our life by diminishing our fears is a slow process. There will be countless setbacks. You will want to surrender in the battle against fear. Do not quit. Press on to greatness!

For The Unicorn Principles, our focus will be on emotional fear — things that cannot physically hurt us but that we fear nonetheless.

Fear of Failure

The most successful people do not fail less, they just do not let failure get in their way. Thomas Edison is the best example of this. His teachers told him that he was too stupid to learn anything. He was fired from his first two jobs for being non-productive. He made 1,000 unsuccessful attempts at inventing the light bulb. Yet, despite these assaults on his psyche, he persevered to incredible success.

Many of us hate to lose. I would like to encourage you to make the shift from hating to lose to loving to win. The math is simple — people who hate to lose risk less, and accordingly, participate in less activities outside of his or her comfort zone. People who love to win accomplish much more. They do not let fear get in the way of success. Imagine what the world would be if Columbus and the other great explorers were driven by a fear of failure.

Redefine Winning and Losing

As discussed in Principle #1 – Walk the Path of Excellence – Perfection is the Enemy of Excellence. You cannot make a big enough impact on your life unless you can accept that you will never be able to achieve perfection. People who strive for perfection never achieve it. No matter who you are or what you do, you are going to make mistakes.

Making a mistake is not losing, failure is not losing, giving up is losing, abandoning The Unicorn Principles is losing.

Systematize the Process

Switching from hating to lose to loving to win is not a license to become a careless swashbuckler. Being careless is not a characteristic of excellence, and it is not a part of the Unicorn Principles. Here are some keys when you are navigating outside of your performance comfort zone.

- Make a plan
- Document the plan
- Get approval of the plan
- Get help
- Build in an ongoing assessment of progress
- Overcommunicate the ongoing status of your project
- Continuously reassess the status of your project with your team
- Have rules to determine when to pull the plug if what you are doing is not working.

Fear of Rejection

Rejection is not failure. If someone is not interested in your idea, concept, product, or service, it is ok. Do not take it personally. I am not aware of anything that is universally loved. Not everyone loves ice cream. Do not be attached to the outcome. The more bravely you confront no's, the more yes's you will get in your life.

Fear of Confrontation

It is challenging to have difficult conversations in an unprepared environment, but ultimately this discomfort will be dramatically superseded by the pain incurred from not addressing critical issues.

Fear of Being Judged

I cannot think of a single time where wondering how someone was going to judge me helped the process. This also applies to fearing embarrassment. Work hard to be the best person you can be, but once you show up, do not let fears of embarrassment or judgement get in the way of your success. Be the best you and stay out of your own way.

Fear of Public Speaking

You are reading this book to become a Unicorn, a distinctive leader in business. As a Unicorn, your career destination will likely include several opportunities to address large groups. The idea of speaking in public can be incredibly frightening to many. I have never seen a situation where a speaker was physically attacked for giving a bad speech. I have seen several instances where the audience went out of their way to help a speaker who was struggling and stammering. Here are some keys for dealing with the fear of public speaking.

- Practice – do it as often as possible. Join speaking groups. Start small. Keep working at it until you get comfortable.
- Watch Others – by watching others, you can learn from the best and discover that almost everyone who delivers a poor speech will recover.

- Relish the opportunity – your objective is to be a standout in the business world. Relish the opportunity to be distinctively better in an area that many fear.

- Forgive mistakes – you are not perfect. Even the best speakers will make mistakes. Forgive yourself, recover, and work to get better. The severe penalties related to public speaking are almost always reserved for the disengaged. Work hard, walk The Unicorn Path, and be better the next time.

Fear of Being Taken Advantage of

This fear is common in every aspect of life but most frequently described in love. I gave her my heart, and she took advantage of me. I am never going to love again; my heart cannot take it.

I have felt hurt and rejection before. Shrinking my life to limit future disappointment made things worse.

People are flawed, and some are evil, but living in fear of disappointment does not help. Live a life of trust and kindness. Shed the disappointments and focus on living a big happy life.

Recover Faster

It is unrealistic to expect that your life will be without emotional fears no matter how well you live this principle. The title of this section is the less you fear, the better your life, not eliminate fear. The primary objective of this principle is reduction of fear. The secondary objective is to recover faster. When fear gets in the way of your path, fight to overcome the related issues. You are human. It is reasonable for you to be less than rational or logical from time to time. Here is a suggested recovery process:

- Identify the fear

- Forgive yourself (you are not perfect)
- Determine how the fear is holding you back/reducing your success
- Get help
- Resolve to reduce fear triggers going forward

Get Good at Breaking Up

Inaction is an especially painful byproduct of fear. We often stay in bad relationships, both personally and professionally, because we fear the pain of breaking up. Rather than risk hurt feelings, people are prone to continue in bad relationships. A huge cause of the alarmingly high 70% employee disengagement rate is people choose to stay with a job they hate. Every day that a person hates his or her job, the passion, purpose, and desire for excellence erodes. Eventually, people wake up one day being part of the zombies in the workplace. Do not let this happen to you. Do not fear the repercussions from breaking up. The consequences of staying in a bad relationship are much greater. If you are not getting the support you need to walk The Unicorn Path, you need to work diligently to fix the problem. If you cannot fix the problem, break up and find a job where your pursuit of excellence is appreciated and rewarded.

Get Help

There is no way to instantaneously eliminate all the emotional fears that you have accumulated throughout your life. This is a major change and as Robin Sharma was previously quoted in Principle #4 "Change is hard at first, messy in the middle, and gorgeous at the end." Get help to make it through the hard and the messy. Here are some examples of help:

- Get your boss involved - Ask he or she to bring to your attention instances where they perceive that fear is inhibiting your progress.
- Get a mentor- Get the benefit from dealing with past experiences
- Get support from your team - The more people who are involved with supporting your success, the easier it is to be successful. Get your teammates on The Unicorn Principles and get a great support team.

The Value of Scarcity

Let others have their careers bogged down due to emotional fears. Walk the path of excellence, accomplish more, stand out from the pack.

PRINCIPLE 13

Set Your Operating Skill on Effective

| *"To be angry is to revenge the faults of others on ourselves."*
– ALEXANDER POPE

ef·fec·tive: /ə'fektiv/: successful in producing a desired or intended result.

What the Disengaged Does:

- They surrender to their natural emotional programming
- They do not see the benefit of self-improvement.
- They see changing their operating system as being phony

EQ is More Valuable Than IQ

EQ is a measure of a person's level of emotional intelligence. EQ refers to a person's ability to perceive, control, evaluate, and express emotions.

IQ represents intelligence quotient. It is derived from a standardized test and measures intellectual attributes such as information processing, knowledge of the world, quantitative reasoning, and memory.

IQ is highly valued in our society and in the workplace. Companies compete to hire the brightest. However, according to Travis Bradberry and Jean Greaves in their book *Emotional Intelligence 2.0*, "people with the highest levels of intelligence (IQ) outperform those with average IQs just 20% of the time, while people with average IQs outperform those with high IQs 70% of the time." This does not diminish the importance of IQ; it just emphasizes the value of being a highly effective person. People with strong EQ's:

- Make others better
- Are great team members
- Are strong contributors to a positive culture.

The Trained Crush the Naturals in EQ

Studies suggest that IQ is static and will not change during a person's life, while EQ is something that we can constantly work to improve.

I toured a well-known tech firm. At lunch in the Company's world-class kitchen with at least 10 different gourmet food stations, I was able to see the incredible distinctions of EQ vs IQ. It was easy to see the incredible IQ of the employees as they moved about, but it was also painfully obvious from the lack of eye contact, poor body language, and the majority of people eating by themselves that there was an extraordinary lack of EQ amongst the employees. The tech employees in the room were undoubtedly on track for financial success, but there were huge deficiencies in happiness and team building. Great food is a wonderful benefit, but the best benefit you can receive is working side by side with people who are geared toward effectiveness and winning as a team.

Developing EQ can be a painful change for bright, socially awkward people, but ultimately the pain of loneliness and sadness will be worse.

- A person with a high EQ and a high IQ can accomplish almost anything
- A person with a high EQ and an average IQ can achieve more than most, including earning the highest levels of financial compensation.
- A person with a high IQ and no regard for EQ can achieve financial success, but it will be likely be limited by poor team support and unhappiness.
- A person with moderate IQ and no interest in EQ is likely to be disengaged and treated like a commodity.

Imagine being able to outperform a genius or an ivy league graduate. EQ is the great equalizer. EQ is virtually ignored in standard education, but with a high EQ, you can dominate your competition and become a distinctively high performer. With great EQ, you can be a key contributor for an incredible team. You can be a star amongst stars.

Treat EQ as a muscle and build a plan to improve your ability to perceive, control, evaluate, and express emotions.

The rest of this section will address aspects of EQ improvement.

Controlling Your Emotions

Our natural internal operating system causes us to react to certain events in standard ways:

When we get very angry, we yell - I used to yell at work. I thought it was a great way to demonstrate passion, commitment, and focus. I thought it was inspirational and motivational. After years of this type of behavior, I realized that it was not working. I was not getting what I wanted by yelling. As a matter of fact, yelling moved me further away from my goal of being a high effective contributor to my Company. The angrier I became, the more people moved away from me. Years later, I learned that I was trading an opportunity for effective communication for a short-term emotional pay-off. Anger is fine. It can be a great motivator, but expressing your anger via yelling is ineffective. Tonality matters more than words in communication. Here are some tips to improve your effectiveness when you are angry:

- Recognize the triggers to anger and fight to resist outbursts
- Do a brief purpose-based affirmation (it is fine to do it silently) such as "yelling won't get me what I want"
- Get help – have a support group to help you make your anger productive
- Master Principle #9 and get great at productive conflict
- Declare your intentions in advance to the people you work with: "I have yelled in the past, and I recognized that it did not help make my teammates better. I am committed to funneling my anger and frustration into positive actions. Sadly, I am not perfect. If I regress and yell again, please call me out. I will appreciate that if you interrupt my yelling, you will do it because you care about me."

Feedback & Feelings

We passionately defend our position, especially if we know we are right – Throughout your career, you will have several opportunities to choose between being right or being effective. This especially happens when people are providing you with feedback. Too often, we debate every aspect of their feedback. There will always be instances where people evaluate you incorrectly, but the inevitable result of being too defensive is that people will stop trying to help you. Forget about getting the last word. Be someone that others want to help rather than someone who knows everything. Here are some tips to avoid being perceived as defensive:

- Carefully chose your battles. If being right does not make you, your team, or your Company better, let go of the debate.
- Keep in mind that being part of a great team is a critical component to Unicorn success.
- Do not get in the way of people trying to help you.
- Understand that the perspectives of others, while not always accurate, are valuable.
- Thank people for caring.
- Use a follow-up session to clean up (clarify) comments.

When we feel slighted, we pout or close down – We all have feelings, and we all get our feelings hurt. It is another part of our natural programming. The problem is how we react. The natural reactions to hurt feelings include pouting, closing down, avoiding the people who caused the problem, and engaging in passive-aggressive behavior. None of these natural reactions make us better, make the team better, or make your Company better. Here are some tips with dealing with hurt feelings at work:

- Recognize that there is no productivity in pouting.
- Accept that people are imperfect and let small slights go.
- Remember that success as a team is based on getting the best from everyone on the team and know that even a silent dispute diminishes optimal effectiveness.

- Since physiology is the most powerful component of communication, it is likely that the person has a pretty good idea of your issues with them.
- Treat unsaid issues as bombs that will explode all over your workplace unless they are defused. This is another great opportunity to display your mastery of Unicorn Principle #9 – Conflict is the Ultimate Competitive Edge.
- Do not vent or engage in any form of passive-aggressive politics. Deal with the transgressor directly. If you need help with the problem, get help, but do not sidestep direct confrontation.

We declare things to be unfair – There are many instances when we do not think that we got what we deserved. This is often attributable to the subjective concept of fairness. One person's version of fairness can differ significantly from another person's version. Some people believe in fairness above all else, while others believe that fairness is a myth that is not required. When we declare something to be unfair, there is an expectation gap problem. We expect one thing and we get another. I cannot recall a single instance where declaring something to be unfair helped the declarant. Here are some hints with dealing with perceived unfairness:

- Resolve to never utter the term "that's unfair." Know that it is unlikely to yield to any effective action.
- Recognize that people are fallible and often make mistakes. These mistakes include overlooking your true value to a project.
- Be someone who is distinctively valuable. Commodities must grapple for their fair share. Be so good that your employer is constantly looking to make your life better.

- Adopt Principle #7 – Clarity is King, and use those skills to always know where you stand and always know what you stand to gain.

We blame other people for our problems – Assuming the role of victim is extremely popular but not very productive. I understand that there are instances in life where you can become a true victim of senseless violence, but in business, the more you blame others, the less likely you are to get others to help you. When you are a victim, you are turning your back on personal accountability. Here are some tips to move from victim status to live a life of personal accountability:

- Passionately embrace personal accountability. When something bad happens at work, your first thought should be what you could have done better.
- Work in an environment where getting better and being excellent is more important than being right.
- Be slow to blame others for problems as it will make the person defensive and make them less likely to contribute to your success going forward.
- Use your communication skills to calmly and effectively communicate the issues.

Perceiving and Evaluating Emotion in Others

I am unfamiliar with mind-reading techniques, but here are techniques to help with evaluating the emotions in others:

Decide to improve – Determine that perceiving and evaluating the emotions of others is distinctively valuable. Pay attention to cues, talk to people who have expertise, and read books.

Build an empathy library – Empathy is the ability to understand how others feel. Empathy is a skill that can be developed. A great way to understand how people feel is to ask people questions about past challenges. This creates a library of experiences that you can apply to current circumstances. We will cover empathy further in Principle #14 You Cannot Be Great if You Are not Good, but empathy is another critical skill that you can develop.

Ask do not guess – When we assume, we act without enough information. Assumptions are mental shortcuts that are hard-wired into our brain. The stakes are high when you are dealing with someone who may be frustrated and disillusioned. Do not take the shortcut of assumptions. Be brave enough to ask tough, clarifying questions in an effective manner. Use your empathy library to craft effective questions in these situations.

Persuasion

The power to persuade someone to do something that he or she would not otherwise do is critical to leadership and effective team dynamics. Too often, people assume that co-workers will do what you ask. In a pervasive environment of disengagement, co-workers will not share your values, and accordingly, they need to be persuaded.

Whys are More Persuasive than Whats and Hows –Bringing back the story of the ant and the elephant, where the ant represents the conscious mind in terms of size and power and the elephant represents the size and power of the subconscious mind. Most of our speech is transactional, dealing with hows and whats. When we speak in a transactional manner, we are speaking directly to the ant (conscious mind). Hows and whats are efficient but not inspiring. To get to the elephant of someone's brain, we need to speak in terms of whys and use imagery. For most people, moving from hows to whats is a tough transition since we have been communicating in a transactional manner our whole lives. Embrace the tools throughout this book to gain the valuable skill of inspirational speech.

How You Say It is More Persuasive Than What You Say - As previously mentioned in Principle #10 – Change the World with Communication, studies have shown that tonality is more influential in communication than the words we use. We also can use tonality to create a better listener. When we use the transactional tonality of everyday speech, the listeners brain processes the information as ordinary and implements a shortcut process. This is the reason why only 20% of most conversations are retained. To enhance listening attention, work to speak in a nurturing tone.

Make it About Them – Another great persuasion tool is to make every personal interaction about them, not about you. If you are focusing on their needs, you will be a better listener. If you are focusing on their needs, you will have a much better conversation.

The Value of Scarcity

There is no complete mastery of EQ. There are infinite opportunities to refine our emotional operating system. Like any distinctive personal skill, you will stumble working to improve your EQ. When you stumble and fall, dust yourself off and get up and keep moving. Forgive yourself. Search for help. Know that just trying to improve your Operating System will make you significantly better than the average employee, and a strong EQ skill set will help you excel in both the business world and your personal life.

PRINCIPLE 14

You Can't Be Great if You Aren't Good

> *"Constant kindness can accomplish much. As the sun makes ice melt, kindness causes misunderstanding, mistrust, and hostility to evaporate."*
> – ALBERT SCHWEITZER

kind·ness: the quality of being friendly, generous, and considerate.

What the Disengaged Does:

- They are content with their current demeanor
- They care more about themselves than they do others
- They gossip and engage in politics
- They see kindness as weakness

In his book, *Good to Great,* Jim Collins says that "Good is the enemy of great." He was right—good is not good enough, you need to strive to be excellent, but this is a different context. The Good of Principle

#14 is kindness, it is about helping others, spreading joy, and creating an environment of happiness.

A happy environment

- Brings out the best of others.
- Attracts high performers that care about quality of life
- Creates a team dynamic that elevates everyone.

Many believe that you can be miserable at work and happy at home, but it is a heck of a lot easier to be happier away from work if you are happy at work.

Happiness is the ultimate benefit and kindness fuels happiness.

Redefine Power

People who believe that kindness is a weakness have never experienced the benefits of a sustainable environment of happy people and a high-performing team. Machiavelli's oft-quoted that "it is better to be feared than loved." His words make great sense for a dictator, but the fact that 70% of all employees are disengaged suggests that it does not work in business. You can whip the horses for short-term results, but if you want long-term success, plant a figurative garden of kindness.

Cruelty and even indifference are enemies of happiness.

Kindness is the cornerstone for building exceptional relationships, winning as a team and achieving happiness.

The best people make the best:

- Employees

- Teammates
- Leaders

Real power comes from:

- Walking The Unicorn Path to become distinctly valuable
- Being able to create a team and galvanize others
- Having the option of being coveted by the marketplace

Unicorn kindness is not being meek and submissive. Unicorns succeed by becoming distinctively valuable and by committing to making others better and happier.

The kindness of a Unicorn involves the courage to:

- Say what needs to be said to speak the truth in an effective manner.
- Work vigorously to improve culture.
- Wage a peaceful war against mediocrity.
- Leave a toxic environment that is determined to be hopeless.

Forget About Quid Pro Quo

There will be countless instances where your kindness will go unrewarded. Favors will go unreturned. Move away from the "what is in it for me" mindset. Remember that perfection is the enemy of excellence. You will never receive perfect rewards. Keep walking the path even if someone responds to your kindness with indifference or cruelty. You are working to become a high performer where your sustained success and happiness will come from the help of others.

There is no need to match someone else's cruelty. It diminishes your effectiveness.

Think of kindness as an investment. There is no such thing as a perfect investment. When you look at stock market graphs, there are ups and downs, but the best investments achieve substantial net gains.

Give More Than You Get

Many think that people who desire to give more than they get are naïve. Science supports the contrary. The more you give, the more you get. The previously mentioned Law of Reciprocity states that when someone does something nice for you, you will have a deep-rooted psychological urge to do something nice in return. In many cases, the reciprocation is more generous than the initial good deed.

There are many forms of giving, such as gifts, food, help, friendship, and emotional support. Gifts do not have to be grand. Even the smallest heartfelt gestures help.

Strive to be a great giver and work to avoid any characterizations of being a taker.

The Battle Against the Disengaged

Remember that 70% of the workforce are characterized as being disengaged in the workplace. In most cases, the disengaged do not see the value of kindness in the workplace. Crowd thinking can be immensely powerful. Do not let the 70% drag you into the pool of indifference or the pit of despair. While they are just following their value systems, know that there is no value in abandoning kindness.

Do not despair when you cannot convert the disengaged into high performers driven by kindness. Some people will not change, and some people do not have the commitment to change. Keep walking your path, and others will join you. I don't know if it is possible to have a mid to large size company with all Unicorns, but I do know that the company with the most Unicorns wins, and an environment of happiness and high performance will attract and develop the most Unicorns.

People Do Business with Those that They Know, Like and Trust

Know, like, and trust are words frequently used in sales, but this phrase matters with co-workers as well. Excelling at consistent, ongoing kindness will build these feelings and make people more likely to work with you.

Build a System of Kindness

Kindness is another area where being a natural is not good enough. A system allows you to reliably duplicate actions, gauge ongoing effectiveness, and refine processes for improvement. There are infinite opportunities to improve kindness and effective human interaction. There are entire books on how to shake hands. Create a list of acts of kindness and work to refine and improve these acts. I recently watched a movie about Fred Rogers (Mr. Rogers), and I was struck by how remarkably kind he was and by how he had developed tools such as swimming and meditation to enhance his kindness.

Authenticity

My favorite definition of authenticity is the act of being raw, naked, and making an unhindered expression of beingness of the soul. It sounds counterintuitive to suggest that you can become authentic since technically, you are being inauthentic by working to be authentic. The metamorphosis starts by working to be someone you want to be, not what you think society wants you to be.

- Be comfortable with yourself and your imperfections
- Courageously tell the truth, no matter how hard it hurts
- Be vulnerable and talk about your mistakes.

It will not be an easy transition, but people love the authentic.

Say Sorry More Often

There is a big push on social media to get people to stop saying that they are sorry because it diminishes a person's power. Everyone makes mistakes, and kind people apologize for their mistakes. Apologies are a component of vulnerability, and they make others like you more and want to help you more.

Empathy

Empathy is the ability to understand and share the feelings of others. Caring about others is the essence of kindness.

Visualize the Future

People are tribal. You may start the process of extreme kindness as a tribe of one, but people will follow. It may take time, and there may be frustrating setbacks in your progress, but visualize a future of being surrounded by a team that is committed to being as kind as you are.

Revenge is a Dish Best Served by Others

Get out of the revenge business. You should expect that people will be brutally unkind to you in the workplace. You cannot be kind if you are looking for revenge on others. Have tough discussions, take legal action if necessary, but forgive if you can. Move to a different job if necessary but do not let the fury of revenge get in the way of your kindness.

Get Help

Like every other component of becoming a Unicorn, it is essential that you get help.

- Tell management about your plan to enhance your kindness and invite them for feedback.
- Ask your co-workers to let you know when they perceive that you are not being kind or to offer advice to improve your kindness.
- Find a kindness mentor.
- Recruit a kindness support group.

The Value of Scarcity

By walking The Unicorn Path you are striving to become a distinctive high-performer. While others are operating on auto pilot, be the one who sees the value of kindness.

PRINCIPLE 15

Tempo and Rhythm Matter in Business Too

| *"Fast Tempo is Essential for Success; Do it, fix it, try it"*
– BRIAN TRACY

| *"The Best Way to Learn is Through the Powerful Force of Rhythm"*
– WOLFGANG AMADEUS MOZART

tem·po: the rate or speed of motion or activity; pace.
rhythm: a strong, regular, repeated pattern of movement or sound.

What the Disengaged Does:

- They Drag Things Out
- They Look Busy to Avoid Doing More
- Procrastinate

Tempo is speed—I just like the word tempo better. Cycle time, the speed that a business accomplishes a cycle is an older business term

179

that still applies today. A company that collects receivables from its customers faster than its competition has the enormous advantage of greater cash. Faster cycle times in production and delivery yield a tremendous increase in customer satisfaction. Fast has always been valuable in business, but speed in individual employee performance is rarely spoken of. I believe that the fear of making mistakes is the governor placed on the speedometers of too many employees.

The Tortoise Never Beats a Unicorn

We all grew up with the story of the tortoise and the hair and the message that slow and steady wins the race. This story has allowed generations to rationalize that being slow was the way to go. If you recall the story, the tortoise was losing by an incredible margin when the rabbit decided to take a nap. The real lesson that I derived from the story is that slow and steady can only beat the actively disengaged. Even workers with a turtle-like pace can beat someone who is sleeping on the job. People who are afraid of making mistakes and people that do not like what they do, are drawn to Slow and Steady. It ratifies their limited production. Slow workers have far less time to help others, have far less time to improve, and almost no chance to walk the path of excellence.

Be Fast in All Things

Turn up your tempo at work. Continuously strive to be faster without being reckless. You cannot be great if:

- You are not prolific.
- You do not have time to help others.
- You do not have the time to improve.
- If you have a fear of failure.

By being fast, you will have many more opportunities to prosper, and you will have more experiences in a far shorter time. The fast beat the slow to the best opportunities, so the deliberate only get the leftovers.

What Unicorn Fast Is

- Working with a Sense of Urgency – treating everything you do as important and immediate
- Being Focused – Fast workers dramatically reduce distractions and stay on task.
- Understanding Your Priorities – It takes great goal orientation and focus to be able to fend off the whirlwind of activities that get in the way of our most important activities.
- Clarity in Roles and Tasks – It is indisputably bad to go fast in the wrong direction. Do not start work before you have a clear idea of what you are doing and what your role is in the project.
- Asking for Help – If you get stuck or you are not clear, ask for help. Nothing will slow you down like trying to power through issues on your own.
- Finishing Far in Advance of Deadlines – Mistakes happen, even with the best of systems. While they might not admit it, the slow and steady make mistakes too. The worst mistakes are when you do not have enough time to fix them. Finishing fast provides more time for review and repair.
- A Passion for Doing More – Being fast allows you to do more and to help more people. The more people you help the more people will help you.

Unicorn fast is not sloppy. Build a system that blends speed with quality. By weaving the 17 principles into a path of excellence, you will eliminate the greatest challenges to speed, sloppiness, and apathy.

Do more, be great, get the rewards that you have earned.

Using Rhythm to Change Your Career

Think about the songs that you sang along to in your car or at concerts. Reflect on how you came to know these songs so well. The easiest answer is that songs live in us due to repetition. The more we hear songs, the more they become part of our memories. I ask you, if we can remember "...That you like pina coladas and getting caught in the rain..." (I know I am dating myself) why can't most people remember the most important aspects of their jobs, such as mission statements and core values? Your teammates will never be able to sing your songs unless they hear them all the time.

Seminars are a great example of the power of rhythm. There are incredible seminars where people pack huge auditoriums and pay large sums to hear incredible messages. Unfortunately, most messages wear off before the charges hit their credit cards. If you do not live the rhythm of a message every day, the message will not weave its way into your daily life.

Most CEOs understand the power of getting employees to buy into their messages. They spend fortunes to develop well-crafted core values and mission statements. They roll out their messages with great fanfare and excitement. They use posters, banners, and paint to spread the word. Despite this magnificent effort, most employees do not know their Company's core values, and more importantly, they do not live them. The biggest reason of disconnection from core values and the ensuing disengagement is a lack of rhythm. Most leaders are not comfortable banging the drum more than a few times a year. Set it and forget it does not drive significant change and quarterly meetings are only slightly more impactful than seminars.

Beat the drum of excellence. It will be uncomfortable, maybe even embarrassing. Fight through the discomfort. Do not worry about people teasing you on your constant repetition. Take it as a compliment. Real discomfort comes from working for bad companies or being part of bad teams. Unicorns are counting on their success coming from the help of others. Talk about the components of The Unicorn Principles every day. The better your teammates understand the path you are walking, the more they will support you.

Get Help

- Get others to spread the word. The more people who beat the drum, the more people will hear it. Encourage others to walk the path of excellence and talk the talk that goes along with it.
- Get support. There is a reason that people rarely talk about what it takes to be excellent and encouraging others to walk the path. It is uncomfortable. People are not used to talking about what it takes to be great. Get a mentor or even a friend to keep you on track, and more importantly, find people who will call you out when your rhythm is lagging.

The Value of Scarcity

Fast is valuable. Being fast and excellent is Unicorn valuable.

The more people understand your values and systems, the more they will be able to help you succeed. The more you talk about it, the more they will understand.

PRINCIPLE 16

Keep Score to Get More

| *"What Gets Measured Gets Done"*
– SLIGHTLY MODIFIED PETER DRUCKER

meas·ure: ascertain the size, amount, or degree of (something) by using an instrument or device marked in standard units or by comparing it with an object of known size.

What the Disengaged Does:

- They hate accountability
- They complain about micro-management
- They try to break the game

When we were growing up, we played games every day. When I ask people when they were growing up if they would have ever played a game without keeping score, the answer has been a universal no. It was inconceivable that as children, we would ever play a game without keeping score. It was critical for us to know where we stood, what we needed to do to win, and the final outcome.

We grow up, we start careers, and we stop keeping score. The stakes are so much higher, yet we shrink from a clear outcome. Here are of my thoughts as to why:

- The game is undefined/the rules are unclear – there are few companies that set the tone with companywide scoring systems. Invoking Principle #7 – Clarity is King, when people do not know the rules, they often guess. When they guess wrong, they receive negative reinforcement. After too many bad guesses and too much negative reinforcement, people stop playing the game.

- Fear of failure – there is too much fear of failure in all aspects of life, and a public display of failure is extra frightening for most. Rather than surrender to your fear, relish the challenge of accountability and enjoy the benefits you will receive from Scoreboard level accountability.

- Disengagement – It is far easier to skate by if there is no performance tracking. The disengaged, by definition, are not interested in improvement. They see no reason for careful tracking and will refer to performance tracking as "micromanagement." You are reading this book to become remarkably better than the disengaged. Do not let them drag you into their pit of despair.

The best performers track everything. Whether you are an Olympic track star or on a diet, the best results come from careful tracking. It is hard to define excellence and dramatic improvement if you are not measuring along the way.

The Unicorn Path

Your goal is to become a Unicorn—someone who will be a standout employee and be a key part of the success of others.

You are walking the path of excellence, and excellence flourishes with measurement. Relish accountability and use it as a foundation of your success.

Characteristics of a Great Scoreboard

1. Your Scoreboard Does Not Need to be Fancy – My favorite example of a simple scoreboard is the oft-told story of Charles Schwab, the steel magnate, not the stockbroker. Over 100 years ago, Schwab was touring one of his low-performing steel plants. He asked his staff how many batches had been processed by the previous shift. The answer was six. Schwab wrote the number 6 in chalk prominently on the plant floor. When the next shift arrived to start work, they looked at the number 6 on the floor. When workers learned what the number represented, they resolved to beat the six. At the end of each shift, the six was replaced with the latest number of batches processed. This simple but effective scoring system drove the plant to become one of Schwab's highest performing locations within a short period of time. As mentioned earlier in the book, white boards or post-it notes are fine. Video screens are even better. Just start keeping score.

2. Your Scoreboard Needs to Be Simple – If something is not simple, it is not sustainable. If it takes too much time or has too much complexity, your scoring system will wilt.

3. Chose Meaningful Numbers – Focus on critical numbers, the kind of numbers that will propel your future. Critical

numbers are often referred to as metrics or Key Performance Indicators (KPIs). The best critical numbers coincide with your goals and your mission. Keep working to improve your metrics. Ask management and people that you work with for help in determining the right numbers.

4. Rise to the Challenge - Do not take the easy way out and select an easy accountability system. Your success comes from improving, not from making an easy number. Play to excel!

5. It Needs to be Public – Do not hide your light under a bushel. Let your journey and progress be seen by everyone you work with. This will enhance your motivation and provide the opportunities for others to help you.

6. Constantly Search for Best Scoreboard practices – Picasso said, "good artists copy, great artists steal." Gladly adopt the best practices of others. Feel free to give attribution.

7. Deploy Benchmarking Whenever Possible – Benchmarking is the comparison of a result against a standard. The pursuit of the 4-minute mile is a great example. A focused pursuit on becoming the first to run a 4-minute mile started in the 1880's. It took until 1954 when Roger Bannister, on a cold day in front of a sparse crowd, became the first person to run a 4-minute mile. Bannister's success made the 4-minute mile a legitimate benchmark and the result was 48 days later John Landy beat Bannister's time, and within a year, 3 more runners ran a 4-minute mile.

8. Consider Using Surveys in Your Scoring – The net promoter score is a simple way to measure feedback. Net Promoter Scores typically involve a one question survey aimed at customer satisfaction. Many of the largest most successful companies in the world use the Net Promoter Score to know where they stand with their customers. Consider surveying your co-workers or key customers on a periodic basis. Make

it an easy 1 question survey. For example, on a scale of 1 to 10, how likely are you to refer someone to work with me? Post the score on your board.

9. Leave Space for a Narrative – Leave space on your scoreboard to write something. It can be celebrating a success, describing the next mountain to climb, or resolving to do better after a setback, but leave a little room to tell your story of walking the path of excellence.

Gamification

Gamification is defined as the application of typical elements of game playing (e.g. point scoring, competition with others, rules of play) to other areas of activity. Giving your work an aspect of a game is a great way to increase performance and have fun along the way.

Get Better at Losing

If you want to win more, you must learn how to lose. Someone who hates to lose will only engage in activities where winning is likely. When we limit our activity, we limit our success. Losing is not failure, quitting is failure. When an unfavorable number on your scoreboard knocks you down, get back up, dust yourself off, and get back on your path to excellence.

Vulnerability

Public disclosure of a loss (or a poor number) on your scoreboard is an incredible act of vulnerability. As a Unicorn, you are working to have others contribute to your success and publicizing your vulnerability is a great way to get others to help you.

It Gets Easier with a Team - Recruit others to post scoreboards. Help them with every aspect of the process. Work with management to develop teamwide scoring.

It is much easier to walk a new path with the help and support of others. Not everyone is interested in what you do. Do not let the haters get in your way.

Competition

Competition is critical to high performance. Roger Bannister was pushed by incredible competition to achieve something that no one had done before. The Wright Brothers were driven by strong competition to become the first in flight, and the space race developed technologies that have changed our lives forever.

Welcome competition, but focus on your personal improvement. If someone is outperforming you, use it as inspiration to do better. Do not spend a minute trying to discredit others to get ahead. Use all your energy to get better.

Remember that you are working to gain incredible success from the help of others. If you work against your competition, you will display characteristics that will drive others away from helping you.

Celebrate the wins of others. Thank others for contributing to your success. Strive every day to be your best.

Get Help

- Ask other competitors for help.
- Adopt the best practices of others.
- Get management/ownership involved in your scorekeeping process.

- Solicit feedback from mentors, peers, and influencers on impactful metrics and scoring presentation.

The Value of Scarcity

Craving accountability and using the results as a springboard for improvement are rare attributes. Walk the Unicorn Path and receive the incredible benefits from being a high-performer.

PRINCIPLE 17

Everybody Says It, Prove It

"Prove it. I'll measure your words against your actions, and from that I will determine your worth."
– JACKIE MORSE KESSLER

prove: demonstrate the truth or existence of (something) by evidence or argument.

What the Disengaged Does:

- They Say If You Hire Me You Will Not Regret It
- They Say I am the Best at What I Do
- They Have No Proof for Their Assertions

Many vendors of goods and services are far from adequate, and some are incompetent or corrupt, yet nearly all of them proclaim that they are the best at what they do. In the interview process, almost every job applicant says they are the best candidate for the job, and if you were to hire them, you would not be sorry. Sadly, most of these hires end up joining the ranks of the disengaged or terminated. The point is that nearly everybody says they are great, and most are not.

If you have read each of the preceding pages of this book, you are serious about doing what it takes to become a Unicorn. Thanks for taking the time to learn about being a Unicorn. Your journey is just starting! Inspirational ideas wash off. Reading this book will not change your life, living this book will change your life.

The objective of The Unicorn Principles are to put you on the path to:

- Becoming an exceptional performer
- Being someone who builds teams and makes others better
- Being a standout who will never have to suffer a frustrating career as a commodity in the workplace.

The Workbook

I have created a workbook designed to allow you to track and score your progress on living each of the 17 Unicorn Principles. Like most things, the more you put into the process, the more you get out.

- Reading this book will help you.
- Embracing a few principals will enrich you.
- Living The Unicorn Principles on a daily basis will make you a premier high-performer.
- Proving that you are walking The Unicorn Path will provide you with incredible opportunities.
- The Unicorn Principles Workbook is your guide for living the Principles and incredible proof of your commitment to excellence.

You can request a workbook by emailing info@UnicornPath.com.

Whether you are looking to improve at your current job or ready to find something new, being able to pull out your workbook and show the work that you are doing to walk The Unicorn path will serve you well.

Use the Unicorn Principles in your Career Search

Think of your career as a partnership where you and your employer will benefit. In an ideal situation, your employer is not doing you a favor by hiring you, they are hiring you to make their Company better. If you are walking The Unicorn Path, companies will be lucky to have you. Embrace The Unicorn Principles in your pursuit of a new career. Seek clarity at all steps. Live your purpose. Do not be traditional, be excellent. Do not fear the rejection.

Find Your Job Do not Let the Job Find You

It is unthinkable to me to allow my resume to be my first impression. Sending your resume in response to job postings should be your last resort. Play the long game and continually look for a job with a company that can propel your career and align with The Unicorn Principles. If you hear something good about a career opportunity, pick up the phone, or better yet, walk into the business and ask for an appointment. If they do not have an open position, still work to get a meeting. If they do not have a spot, ask for permission to follow-up. By deploying The Unicorn Principles in your job search, you will get the career you deserve.

Why Do You Want to Work Here?

This is a question frequently asked during interviews. You're committed to Unicorn Principle #2 Purpose is a Superpower. You want to work at a job that aligns with your purpose. Here is my recommended response to the question, why do you want to work here? I do not know if I do. I am excited to be here. I have heard great things about this Company. I am happy to provide you with any information for you to make the right decision, but I am also here to determine whether your Company aligns with my mission and core values.

Rejection Is not your Enemy

If you get rejected in the career search process, it may leave a bruise, but it will not kill you. To flourish in this process, you need to know the true enemies:

- Companies that treat employees like commodities
- Companies that do not have strategic growth plans to support your career growth
- Companies that do not have strong core values

The real pain comes from working at a job that you hate. To get the best job, it is likely that you will encounter some rejection.

Get Help

As you are walking the Unicorn path, you are building a strong support group of mentors, managers, co-workers, and friends. Give these people a chance to help your career.

- Ask them to post testimonials on Linked In or other online resources.
- Ask them to be on the lookout for opportunities that might fit your path, skillset and passion.
- Ask them to provide pro-active (pre-interview) referrals.

The Value of Scarcity

Real improvement comes from commitment, repetition and support. If you want to establish incredible value in the business world, use The Unicorn Principles Workbook as a map to walk the path every day.

Made in the USA
Las Vegas, NV
29 September 2021